PAT SLOAN'S

Holiday Celebrations

17 Quilts and More for
6 Seasonal Occasions

Martingale
Create with Confidence

Pat Sloan's Holiday Celebrations:
17 Quilts and More for 6 Seasonal Occasions
© 2021 by Pat Sloan

Martingale®
18939 120th Ave. NE, Ste. 101
Bothell, WA 98011-9511 USA
ShopMartingale.com

Printed in Hong Kong
26 25 24 23 22 21   8 7 6 5 4 3 2

Library of Congress Cataloging-in-Publication Data is available upon request.

ISBN: 978-1-68356-131-6

MISSION STATEMENT

We empower makers who use fabric and yarn to make life more enjoyable.

CREDITS

PUBLISHER AND
CHIEF VISIONARY OFFICER
Jennifer Erbe Keltner

CONTENT DIRECTOR
Karen Costello Soltys

DESIGN MANAGER
Adrienne Smitke

TECHNICAL EDITOR
Nancy Mahoney

PRODUCTION MANAGER
Regina Girard

COPY EDITOR
Durby Peterson

BOOK DESIGNER
Angie Haupert Hoogensen

ILLUSTRATOR
Sandy Loi

COVER DESIGNER
Mia Mar

PHOTOGRAPHER
Brent Kane

SPECIAL THANKS
Some of the photography for this book was taken at the home of Cliff and Rosemary Bailey in Snohomish, Washington.

CONTENTS

Years ago, I saw a stitchery with the saying "Happy Everything," and it included holiday images from Saint Patrick's Day to Christmas. The phrase pops into my head each time I look for that next box of holiday decorations and quilts.

I'm thrilled to design a year's worth of quilted holiday projects. My love of holiday decorating runs deep, and I know exactly who I got my obsession from: Granny. My dad's mom. Granny decorated for every holiday. She and Pappy had a basement full of stored decorations ranging from gorgeous Easter baskets and American flags to a huge painted Santa in a sled for the front lawn. Their basement was my favorite place to play as a kid.

Making a holiday feel special is something I do for myself. I'm more cheerful and happy when my space is decorated. It doesn't take much to transform a room. Add a table runner along with holiday pillows. Hang a special quilt on the wall or drape a quilt on the sofa. Making and then enjoying holiday decorations enriches the season.

I like to put up the main pieces a few weeks prior to the holiday. I set out Valentine's Day adornments in mid-January. Thanksgiving motifs come out in early November, right after Halloween. That way I enjoy the decorations for more than just a few days.

With the projects in *Pat Sloan's Holiday Celebrations*, you'll transform your holidays with table runners, pillows, totes, and quilts. I can't wait to see what you create!

Join my Facebook group, Quilt Along with Pat Sloan, and share your photos with me. It's time to have a Happy Everything Year!

Love and kisses,

I love to
Pat ♥

Be My Always

Were you the one who ended your notes with XOXO and always dotted the letter i with a heart? Yep, me too. A heart is one of my all-time favorite shapes, and Valentine's Day is a wonderful time to bring out all the heart motifs. I display heart quilts and pillows in late January and keep them out through the middle of March.

Lap Quilt

FINISHED QUILT: 65½" × 77"
FINISHED BLOCK: 18" × 16"

Materials

Yardage is based on 42"-wide fabric.

¼ yard *each* of 9 assorted red prints for blocks and sashing

3¼ yards of white solid for blocks, sashing, and borders

⅓ yard *each* of 3 assorted pink prints for blocks and sashing

¼ yard *each* of 4 assorted pink prints for blocks and sashing

⅓ yard of raspberry print for middle border

⅝ yard of pink solid for binding

4⅝ yards of fabric for backing

72" × 83" piece of batting

Cutting

All measurements include ¼" seam allowances.

From *1* of the red prints, cut:
- 2 strips, 2½" × 42"; crosscut into:
  - 2 rectangles, 2½" × 4½"
  - 14 squares, 2½" × 2½"
  - 5 squares, 2" × 2"
- 1 strip, 2" × 42"; crosscut into 19 squares, 2" × 2"

From *each of 3* red prints, cut:
- 3 strips, 2½" × 42"; crosscut into:
  - 4 rectangles, 2½" × 4½" (12 total)
  - 28 squares, 2½" × 2½" (84 total)

From *each of 5* red prints, cut:
- 2 strips, 2½" × 42"; crosscut into:
  - 2 rectangles, 2½" × 4½" (10 total)
  - 14 squares, 2½" × 2½" (70 total)

From the white solid, cut:
- 23 strips, 2½" × 42"; crosscut into:
  - 24 rectangles, 2½" × 8½"
  - 24 rectangles, 2½" × 6½"
  - 60 rectangles, 2½" × 4½"
  - 72 squares, 2½" × 2½"
- 23 strips, 2" × 42"; crosscut 9 *of the strips* into:
  - 6 strips, 2" × 17"
  - 3 strips, 2" × 15½"
  - 4 strips, 2" × 15"
  - 4 strips, 2" × 13½"

From *each* of the ⅓-yard cuts of pink prints, cut:
- 4 strips, 2½" × 42"; crosscut into:
  - 4 rectangles, 2½" × 8½" (12 total; 1 will be extra)
  - 6 rectangles, 2½" × 4½" (18 total)
  - 20 rectangles, 2½" × 3½" (60 total)
  - 1 square, 2" × 2" (3 total; 1 will be extra)

From *1* of the ¼-yard cuts of pink prints, cut:
- 2 strips, 2½" × 42"; crosscut into:
  - 4 rectangles, 2½" × 8½"
  - 2 rectangles, 2½" × 4½"
  - 10 squares, 2½" × 2½"
  - 1 square, 2" × 2"

Continued on page 8

Continued from page 7

From *1* of the ¼-yard cuts of pink prints, cut:
- 2 strips, 2½" × 42"; crosscut into:
    4 rectangles, 2½" × 8½"
    2 rectangles, 2½" × 4½"
    10 squares, 2½" × 2½"
    1 square, 2" × 2"

From *1* of the ¼-yard cuts of pink prints, cut:
- 3 strips, 2½" × 42"; crosscut into:
    6 rectangles, 2½" × 8½"
    10 squares, 2½" × 2½"
    1 square, 2" × 2"

From *1* of the ¼-yard cuts of pink prints, cut:
- 2 strips, 2½" × 42"; crosscut into:
    5 rectangles, 2½" × 8½"
    2 rectangles, 2½" × 4½"
    1 square, 2" × 2"

From the raspberry print, cut:
- 7 strips, 1½" × 42"

From the pink solid, cut:
- 8 strips, 2¼" × 42"

Making the A Blocks

Press seam allowances in the directions indicated by the arrows.

1 For each block, select the following pieces:

- Two white 2½" × 8½" rectangles
- Two white 2½" × 6½" rectangles
- Five white 2½" × 4½" rectangles
- Six white 2½" squares
- Matching set of two red 2½" × 4½" rectangles and 14 red 2½" squares
- Matching set of two pink 2½" × 4½" rectangles and 10 pink 2½" × 3½" rectangles
- Matching set of five pink 2½" squares from a different pink print

2 Arrange and sew the pieces into nine columns as shown. Join the columns to make a block measuring 18½" × 16½", including seam allowances. Make six.

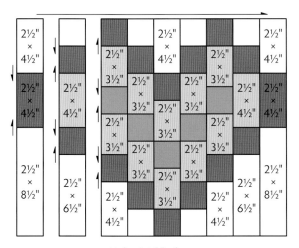

Make 6 A blocks,
18½" × 16½".

Making the B Blocks

1 For each block, select the following pieces:

- Two white 2½" × 8½" rectangles
- Two white 2½" × 6½" rectangles
- Five white 2½" × 4½" rectangles
- Six white 2½" squares
- Matching set of two red 2½" × 4½" rectangles and 14 red 2½" squares
- Five assorted pink 2½" × 8½" rectangles
- Two different pink 2½" × 4½" rectangles

2 Arrange and sew the pieces into nine columns as shown. Join the columns to make a block measuring 18½" × 16½", including seam allowances. Make six.

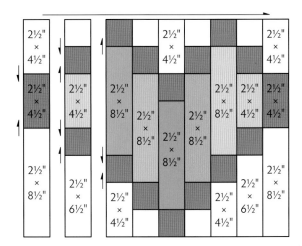

Make 6 B blocks,
18½" × 16½".

2 Sew a red 2" square to a white 2" × 17" strip. Make six C strips measuring 2" × 18½", including seam allowances. Sew a red 2" square to each end of a white 2" × 15½" strip. Make three D strips measuring 2" × 18½", including seam allowances.

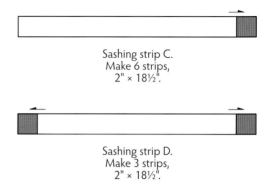

Sashing strip C.
Make 6 strips,
2" × 18½".

Sashing strip D.
Make 3 strips,
2" × 18½".

Assembling the Quilt Top

Refer to the quilt assembly diagram on page 11 as needed throughout.

1 Lay out the A and B blocks in four rows, alternating them in each row and from row to row. Place A sashing strips between the blocks in the top and bottom rows. Place B sashing strips between the blocks in the two center rows. Sew the blocks and strips into rows.

2 Join two C sashing strips, two pink 2" squares, and one D sashing strip to make a sashing row measuring 2" × 57½", including seam allowances. Make three sashing rows.

3 Join the block and sashing rows to make a quilt top measuring 57½" × 69", including seam allowances.

4 Join the white 2"-wide strips end to end. From the pieced strip, cut two 77"-long strips, two 72"-long strips, two 62½"-long strips, and two 57½"-long strips.

5 Sew the white 2" × 57½" strips to the top and bottom of the quilt top. Sew the white 2" × 72" strips to opposite sides of the quilt top, which should be 60½" × 72", including seam allowances.

Making the Sashing Strips

1 Sew a red 2" square to a white 2" × 15" strip. Make four A strips measuring 2" × 16½", including seam allowances. Sew a red 2" square to each end of a white 2" × 13½" strip. Make four B strips measuring 2" × 16½", including seam allowances.

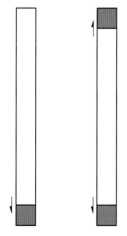

Sashing strip A.   Sashing strip B.
Make 4 strips,   Make 4 strips,
2" × 16½".   2" × 16½".

6 Join the raspberry 1½"-wide strips end to end. From the pieced strip, cut two 74"-long strips and two 60½"-long strips. Sew the shorter strips to the top and bottom of the quilt top. Sew the longer strips to opposite sides of the quilt top, which should be 62½" × 74", including seam allowances.

7 Sew the white 2" × 62½" strips to the top and bottom of the quilt top. Sew the white 2" × 77" strips to opposite sides of the quilt top, which should be 65½" × 77".

Finishing the Quilt

For more details on any finishing steps, visit ShopMartingale.com/HowtoQuilt for free downloadable information.

1 Layer the quilt top with batting and backing; baste the layers together.

2 Quilt by hand or machine. The quilt shown is machine quilted with a heart shape in each block. Various motifs are quilted inside each heart motif. The block background is quilted with curved lines and loops. A row of circles is stitched in each sashing strip. A continuous heart motif is quilted in the borders.

3 Use the pink solid 2¼"-wide strips to make binding and then attach the binding to the quilt.

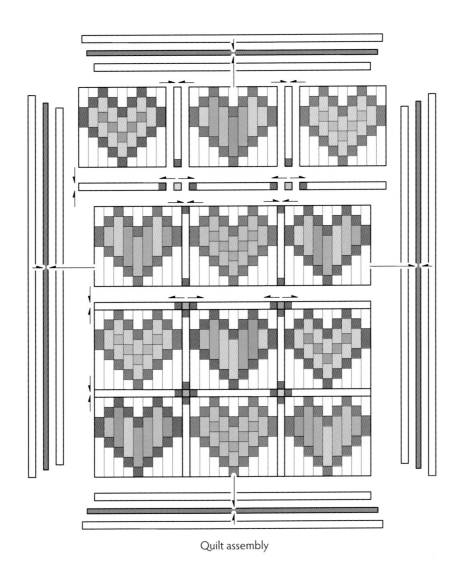

Quilt assembly

Valentine Pillow

 FINISHED PILLOW: 18" × 18"
FINISHED BLOCK: 10" × 10"

Materials

Yardage is based on 42"-wide fabric. Fat eighths measure 9" × 21".

⅞ yard of red print for block, border, and pillow back

2 fat eighths, 1 *each* of 2 different white prints (A and B) for block

⅝ yard of white solid for backing

20" × 20" piece of batting

18" × 18" pillow form

Cutting

All measurements include ¼" seam allowances.

From the red print, cut:
• 2 strips, 4½" × 42"; crosscut into:
    2 strips, 4½" × 18½"
    2 strips, 4½" × 10½"
• 2 rectangles, 13½" × 18½"
• 2 squares, 5½" × 5½"
• 4 squares, 2½" × 2½"

From white print A, cut:
• 2 rectangles, 2½" × 10½"
• 2 rectangles, 2½" × 5½"

From white print B, cut:
• 2 rectangles, 2½" × 10½"

From the white solid, cut:
• 1 square, 20" × 20"

Making the Pillow Front

Press seam allowances in the directions indicated by the arrows.

1   Draw a diagonal line from corner to corner on the wrong side of the red 2½" squares. Place a marked square on one end of a white A 2½" × 5½" rectangle, right sides together. Sew on the marked line. Trim the excess corner fabric ¼" from the stitched line. Place a marked square on the other end of the rectangle, noting the orientation of the marked line. Sew and trim as before to make a unit measuring 2½" × 5½", including seam allowances. Make two units.

Make 2 units,
2½" × 5½".

2   Sew together the two units from step 1 to make the top row. Join the top row, the A 2½" × 10½"

rectangles, and the B rectangles, alternating the A and B rectangles. Make one unit measuring 10½" square, including seam allowances.

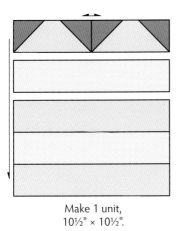

Make 1 unit,
10½" × 10½".

3 Draw a diagonal line from corner to corner on the wrong side of the red 5½" squares. Place a marked square on the lower-left corner of the unit from step 2, right sides together. Sew on the marked line. Trim the excess corner fabric ¼" from the stitched line. Place a marked square on the lower-right corner of the unit, noting the orientation of the marked line. Sew and trim as before to make a block measuring 10½" square, including seam allowances.

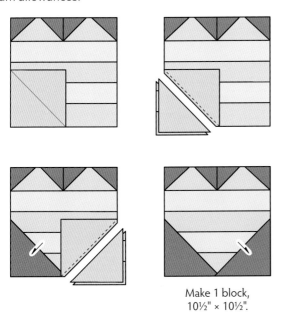

Make 1 block,
10½" × 10½".

4 Sew the red 4½" × 10½" strips to the top and bottom of the block. Sew the red 4½" × 18½" strips to the left and right edges to make the pillow front, which should be 18½" square, including seam allowances.

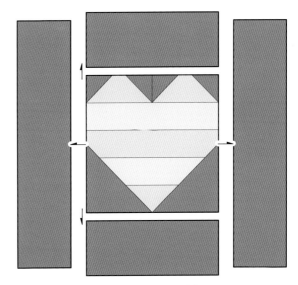

Pillow-front assembly

↳ Decorating with pillows immediately changes the mood in a room. Amp up the love with heart-inspired pillows in red and white.

Assembling the Pillow

1 Layer the pillow front with batting and the white solid square; baste the layers together. Quilt by hand or machine. The pillow shown is machine quilted from side to side with evenly spaced lines using a decorative wavy stitch.

2 Trim the pillow front to 18½" square, including seam allowances.

3 To make the pillow back, fold over ¼" on one 18½" edge of both red 13½" × 18½" rectangles, and then fold over ¼" again. Press and machine stitch along the folded edge.

4 Overlap the pillow backs on top of the pillow front, right sides together and raw edges aligned. Pin and then stitch around the perimeter using a ¼" seam allowance.

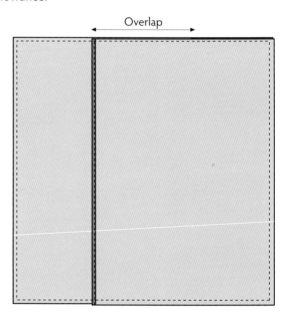

Overlap

5 Turn the pillow right side out. Insert the pillow form.

For a different look, use a white print instead of a red print for the background and border. Then choose two red prints to make the heart shape.

VALENTINE'S DAY

Hello, Luv!

With just a handful of 5" squares, you can create a super cute table mat for your Valentine's Day decorating! With just four blocks, this little quilt comes together quickly and also makes a perfect present to warm the heart of someone you love.

Materials

Yardage is based on 42"-wide fabric.

4 pairs of squares, 5" × 5" *each,* of assorted black prints for blocks

4 pairs of squares, 5" × 5" *each,* of assorted red and pink prints for blocks (referred to collectively as "pink")

½ yard of white print for blocks and border

¼ yard of black solid for binding

¾ yard of fabric for backing

26" × 26" piece of batting

4 red and 4 black buttons, ³⁄₁₆" to 1" in diameter, for block centers

3 red and 2 black novelty buttons, ³⁄₁₆" to 1" in diameter, for upper-right corner (I used heart- and flower-shaped buttons.)

Cutting

All measurements include ¼" seam allowances.

From the white print, cut:
- 3 strips, 3" × 42"; crosscut into 32 squares, 3" × 3"
- 2 strips, 2" × 42"; crosscut *each* strip into:
    1 strip, 2" × 21½" (2 total)
    1 strip, 2" × 18½" (2 total)

From the black solid, cut:
- 3 strips, 2¼" × 42"

LEARN MORE

You'll find more information about my sew-and-flip techniques in my book Pat Sloan's Teach Me to Sew Triangles *(Martingale, 2015).*

Making the Blocks

Press seam allowances in the directions indicated by the arrows.

1 Draw a diagonal line from corner to corner on the wrong side of the white 3" squares. Place marked squares on opposite corners of a black 5" square. Sew on the marked line. Trim the excess corner fabric ¼" from the stitched line. Make eight black units measuring 5" square, including seam allowances.

Make 8 units,
5" × 5".

2 Repeat step 1 using the remaining marked squares and the pink 5" squares to make eight units.

Make 8 units,
5" × 5".

3 Lay out two pairs of matching black units in two rows, noting the orientation of the units. Sew the units into rows. Join the rows to make an × block. Make two blocks measuring 9½" square, including seam allowances.

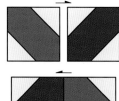
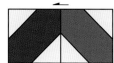
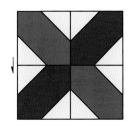

Make 2 X blocks,
9½" × 9½".

4 Lay out two pairs of matching pink units in two rows, noting the orientation of the units. Sew the units into rows. Join the rows to make an O block. Make two blocks measuring 9½" square, including seam allowances.

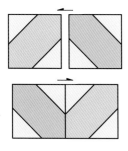 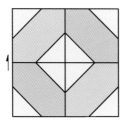

Make 2 O blocks,
9½" × 9½".

Assembling the Table Mat

1 Lay out the X and O blocks in two rows of two blocks each as shown in the table-mat assembly diagram below. Sew the blocks into rows. Join the rows to make a table mat measuring 18½" square, including seam allowances.

2 Sew the white 2" × 18½" strips to the top and bottom of the table mat. Sew the white 2" × 21½" strips to opposite sides of the table mat, which should be 21½" square.

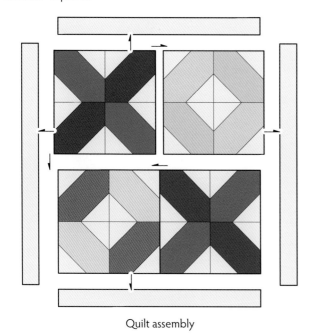

Quilt assembly

Finishing the Table Mat

For more details on any finishing steps, visit ShopMartingale.com/HowtoQuilt for free downloadable information.

1 Layer the table-mat top with batting and backing; baste the layers together.

2 Quilt by hand or machine. The table mat shown is machine quilted with loops in the background of the blocks. Straight lines are stitched across the center of each × block, and wavy lines are stitched around the center of each O block. A wavy line with loops is quilted in the outer border.

3 Use the black 2¼"-wide strips to make binding and then attach the binding to the table mat.

4 Sew one red and one black button in the center of each block. Sew the remaining buttons in the upper-right corner as shown on page 15.

Chubby Carrots

Easter reminds me so much of my Granny and her many wonderful holiday items, including a bright orange carrot-shaped candy dish. Naturally, my decorations have to include carrots. Chubby Carrots is the perfect setting to display an abundant Easter basket or two.

Table Runner

FINISHED QUILT: 18½" × 46½"
FINISHED CARROT BLOCK: 4" × 10"
FINISHED CHECKERBOARD BLOCK: 16" × 22"

Materials

Yardage is based on 42"-wide fabric. Fat eighths measure 9" × 21".

⅞ yard of white print for blocks, sashing, and border

3 fat eighths of assorted orange prints for Carrot blocks

½ yard of green check for Carrot blocks and binding

⅛ yard *each* of 3 different olive prints for Checkerboard block

1½ yards of fabric for backing

25" × 53" piece of batting

Cutting

All measurements include ¼" seam allowances.

From the white print, cut:
- 1 strip, 3" × 42"; crosscut into 6 squares, 3" × 3"
- 6 strips, 2½" × 42"; crosscut *3 of the strips* into:
    - 4 strips, 2½" × 10½"
    - 12 squares, 2½" × 2½"
- 6 strips, 1½" × 42"; crosscut *3 of the strips* into:
    - 2 strips, 1½" × 18½"
    - 2 strips, 1½" × 16½"
    - 12 squares, 1½" × 1½"

From *each* of the orange prints, cut:
- 2 rectangles, 4½" × 8½" (6 total)

From the green check, cut:
- 1 strip, 3" × 42"; crosscut into 6 squares, 3" × 3"
- 4 strips, 2¼" × 42"

From *each* of the olive prints, cut:
- 1 strip, 2½" × 42" (3 total)

Making the Carrot Blocks

Press seam allowances in the directions indicated by the arrows.

1 Draw a diagonal line from corner to corner on the wrong side of the white 2½" and 1½" squares. Place a marked 2½" square on the bottom left corner of an orange rectangle. Sew on the marked line. Trim the excess corner fabric ¼" from the stitched line. Place a marked 2½" square on the bottom right corner of the rectangle. Sew and trim as before to make a unit measuring 4½" × 8½", including seam allowances. Make six units.

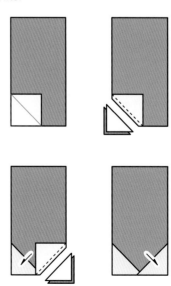

Make 6 units,
4½" × 8½".

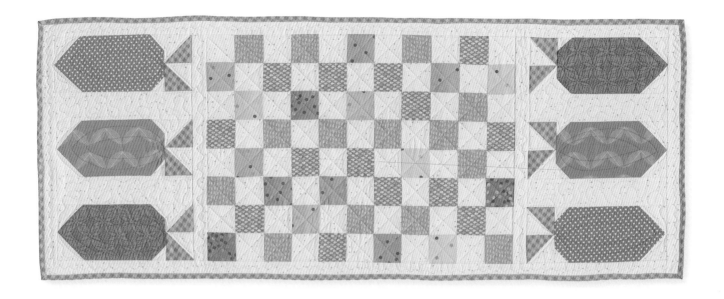

2 Place marked white 1½" squares on the top corners of the unit from step 1. Repeat step 1 to sew and trim. The carrot units should measure 4½" × 8½", including seam allowances. Make six units.

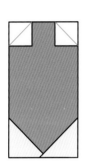 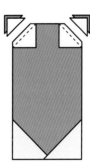

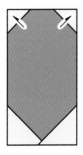

Make 6 units,
4½" × 8½".

3 Draw a diagonal line from corner to corner on the wrong side of the white 3" squares. Layer a marked square on a green 3" square, right sides together. Sew ¼" from both sides of the drawn line. Cut the unit apart on the marked line to make two half-square-triangle units. Trim the units to 2½" square, including seam allowances. Make 12 units.

Make 12 units.

4 Join two half-square-triangle units, noting the orientation of the units, to make a top unit. Sew a top unit to each carrot unit to make six Carrot blocks measuring 4½" × 10½", including seam allowances.

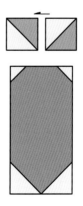 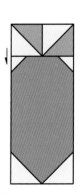

Make 6 Carrot blocks,
4½" × 10½".

EASTER

Making the Checkerboard Block

1 Sew a white 2½"-wide strip to the long side of an olive strip to make a strip set measuring 4½" × 42". Make three strip sets. Cut the strip sets into 44 segments, 2½" × 4½", including seam allowances.

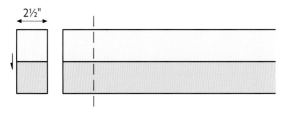

Make 3 strip sets, 4½" × 42".
Cut 44 segments, 2½" × 4½".

2 Lay out the segments in 11 rows of four segments each, rotating the segments in every other row. Sew the segments into rows. Join the rows to make a Checkerboard block measuring 16½" × 22½", including seam allowances.

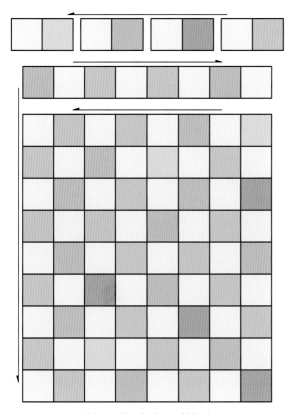

Make 1 Checkerboard block,
16½" × 22½".

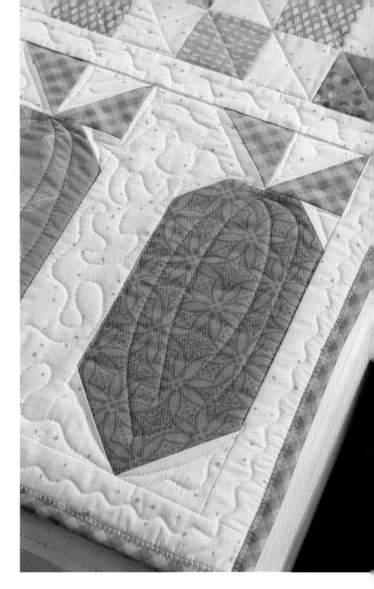

Assembling the Table-Runner Top

Refer to the table-runner assembly diagram at right as needed throughout.

1   Join three Carrot blocks and two white 2½" × 10½" strips to make a carrot row. Make two rows measuring 10½" × 16½", including seam allowances.

2   Lay out the carrot rows from step 1, the white 1½" × 16½" strips, and the Checkerboard block, noting the orientation of the carrot rows. Join the pieces to make a table-runner center measuring 16½" × 44½", including seam allowances.

3   Join the remaining white 1½" × 42" strips end to end. From the pieced strip, cut two 44½"-long strips and sew them to opposite sides of the table runner. Sew the white 1½" × 18½" strips to the ends of the table runner, which should be 18½" × 46½".

Finishing the Table Runner

For more details on any finishing steps, visit ShopMartingale.com/HowtoQuilt for free downloadable information.

1   Layer the table-runner top with batting and backing; baste the layers together.

2   Quilt by hand or machine. The table runner shown is machine quilted with diagonal crosshatching in the checkerboard. A meandering design is stitched in the background of the carrot row and curved lines are stitched in the carrots. Wavy lines are quilted in the border.

3   Use the green check 2¼"-wide strips to make binding and then attach the binding to the quilt.

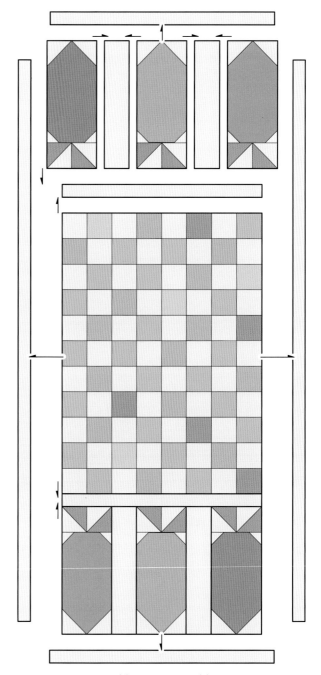

Table-runner assembly

Bunny Hop Pillow

FINISHED PILLOW: 16" × 16"
FINISHED BLOCK: 12" × 12"

Materials

Yardage is based on 42"-wide fabric.

⅝ yard of green print A for block, border, and pillow back

2 strips, 3" × 16" *each*, of different green prints (B and C) for block

7" × 7" square of green print D for leaves

3 strips, 3" × 16" *each*, of assorted yellow prints (A–C) for block

9" × 14" rectangle of yellow print D for oval

2" × 3" rectangle of yellow print E for flower center

4" × 8" rectangle of orange print for flower and ribbon

⅝ yard of white solid for bunny and pillow-top backing

20" × 20" piece of batting

16" × 16" pillow form

¾ yard of 16"-wide paper-backed fusible web

50-weight thread in colors to match appliqués

Cutting

All measurements include ¼" seam allowances.

From green print A, cut:
- 1 strip, 12½" × 42"; crosscut into 2 rectangles, 12½" × 16½"
- 2 strips, 2½" × 42"; crosscut into:
    2 strips, 2½" × 16½"
    2 strips, 2½" × 12½"
    6 squares, 2½" × 2½"

From *each* of green prints B and C, cut:
- 6 squares, 2½" × 2½" (12 total)

From *each* of yellow prints A–C, cut:
- 6 squares, 2½" × 2½" (18 total)

From the white solid, cut:
- 1 square, 20" × 20"

Making the Pillow Front

You can learn more about my fusible-appliqué techniques in my book *Pat Sloan's Teach Me to Appliqué* (Martingale, 2015). Press seam allowances in the directions indicated by the arrows.

1   Lay out the green and yellow squares in six rows of six squares each, alternating the colors in each row and from row to row. Sew the squares into rows. Join the rows to make a block measuring 12½" square, including seam allowances.

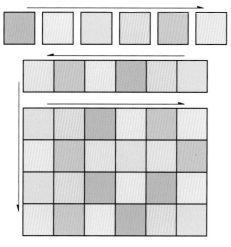

Make 1 block,
12½" × 12½".

2   Sew the green A 2½" × 12½" strips to opposite sides of the block. Sew the green A 2½" × 16½" strips to the top and bottom to make the pillow front, which should be 16½" square, including seam allowances.

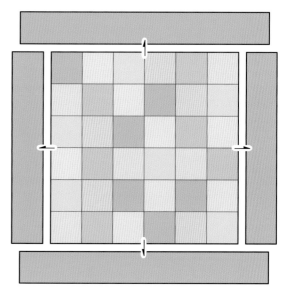

Pillow-front assembly

3   Using the patterns on pages 26 and 27, trace each shape the number of times indicated onto the fusible web. Roughly cut out each shape, about ½" beyond the drawn line. For larger shapes, such as the rabbit and oval, cut through the excess web around the shape, through the marked line, and into the interior of the shape. Cut away the excess fusible web on the *inside* of the shape, leaving about ¼" inside the drawn line.

4   Position the fusible-web shapes on the fabrics indicated on the patterns. Fuse as instructed by the manufacturer. Cut out the shapes on the marked line and remove the paper backing from each shape.

HOP TO IT!

My Easter decorating isn't complete until the bunnies come out to play. A bright orange ribbon adds the finishing touch for this frolicking little fellow.

This checkerboard pillow with fusible appliqué is so quick to make, you may want to stitch several tops and quilt them for use as place mats at your Easter brunch.

5 Referring to the appliqué placement diagram, position the prepared appliqué shapes on the pillow front starting with the oval.

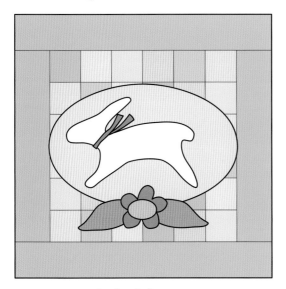

Appliqué placement

6 Fuse the appliqués in place. Blanket-stitch around the outer edge of each shape using matching thread.

Assembling the Pillow

1 Layer the pillow front with batting and the white solid square; baste the layers together. Quilt by hand or machine. The pillow shown is machine quilted with wavy lines in the background. The appliqués are outline stitched and straight lines are stitched in the border strips.

2 Trim the pillow front to 16½" square, including seam allowances.

3 To make the pillow back, fold over ¼" on one 16½" edge of both green 12½" × 16½" rectangles, and then fold over ¼" again. Press and machine stitch along the folded edge.

4 Referring to the diagram on page 14, overlap the pillow backs on top of the pillow front, right sides together and raw edges aligned. Pin and then stitch around the perimeter using a ¼" seam allowance.

5 Turn the pillow right side out. Insert the pillow form.

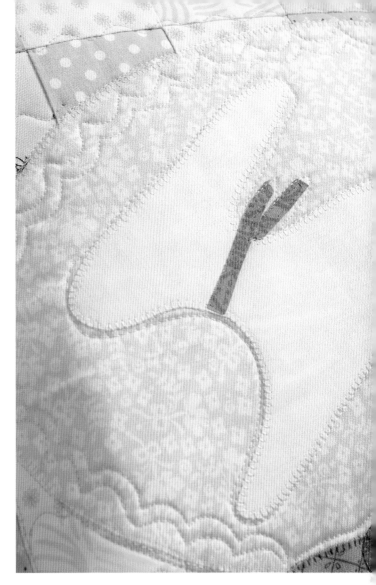

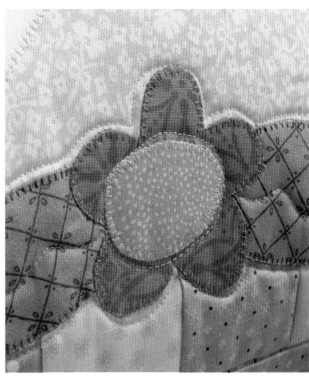

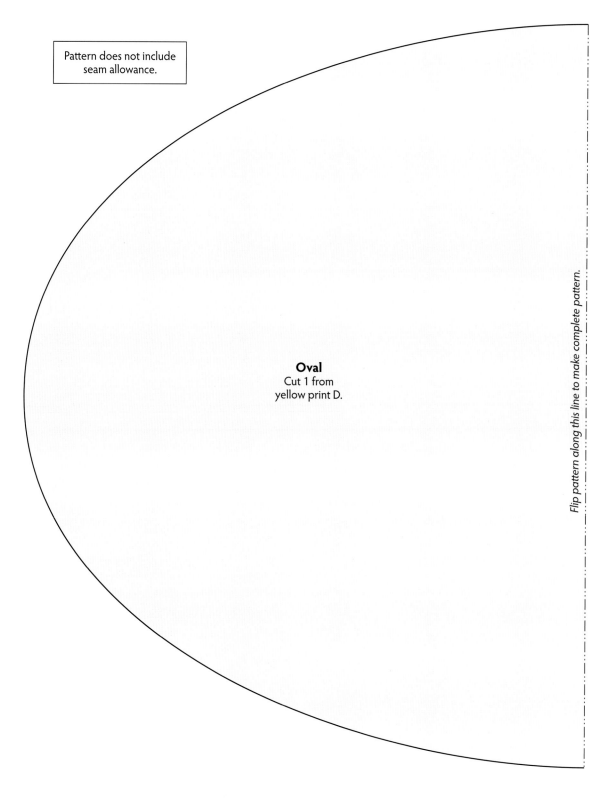

Pattern does not include
seam allowance.

Oval
Cut 1 from
yellow print D.

Flip pattern along this line to make complete pattern.

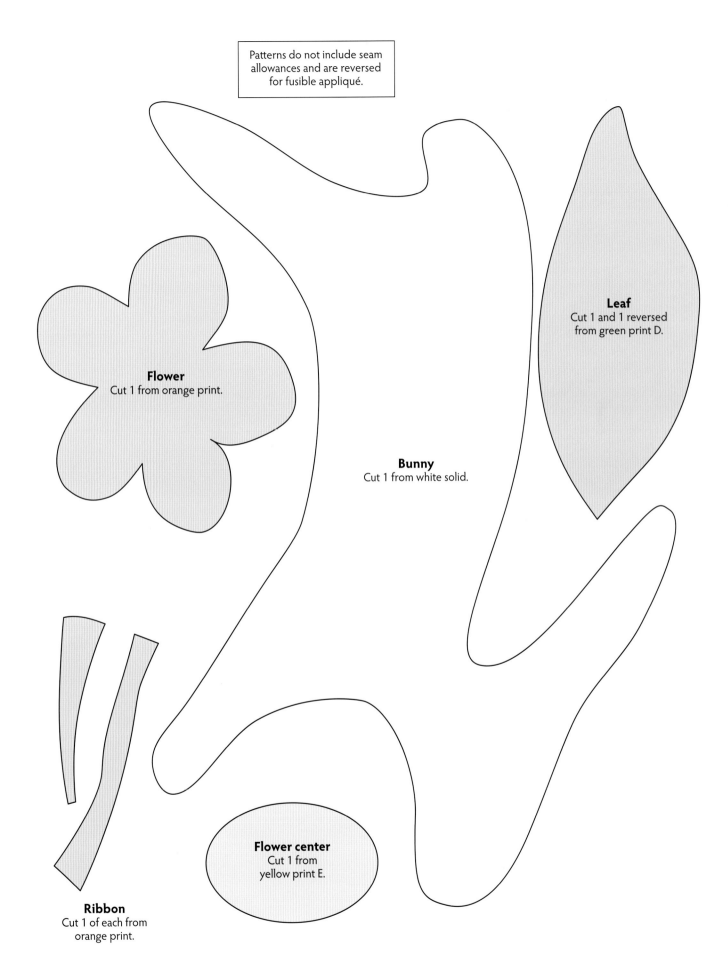

Patterns do not include seam allowances and are reversed for fusible appliqué.

Leaf
Cut 1 and 1 reversed from green print D.

Flower
Cut 1 from orange print.

Bunny
Cut 1 from white solid.

Flower center
Cut 1 from yellow print E.

Ribbon
Cut 1 of each from orange print.

Easter Basket Coasters

FINISHED COASTER: 7½" × 7½"
FINISHED BLOCK: 6" × 6"

Materials

Yardage is based on 42"-wide fabric. Yields 4 coasters.

⅜ yard of white print for blocks and border

½ yard of green dot for blocks and binding

3" × 12" rectangle of yellow print for blocks

3" × 10" rectangle of orange print for blocks*

4 squares, 10" × 10" *each*, of fabric for backing

4 squares, 10" × 10" *each*, of batting

*If you want to fussy cut a motif, as I did, you may need more fabric.

Cutting

All measurements include ¼" seam allowances.

From the white print, cut:
- 1 strip, 2½" × 42"; crosscut into 8 squares, 2½" × 2½"
- 2 strips, 2" × 42"; crosscut into:
    8 rectangles, 2" × 3½"
    20 squares, 2" × 2"
- 3 strips, 1" × 42"; crosscut into:
    8 strips, 1" × 7½"
    8 strips, 1" × 6½"

From the green dot, cut:
- 4 strips, 2¼" × 42"
- 4 squares, 2½" × 2½"
- 8 rectangles, 2" × 3½"

From the yellow print, cut:
- 4 squares, 2½" × 2½"

From the orange print, cut:
- 4 squares, 2" × 2"

Making the Coasters

Press seam allowances in the directions indicated by the arrows.

1. Draw a diagonal line from corner to corner on the wrong side of the white 2½" squares. Layer a marked square on a green square, right sides together. Sew ¼" from both sides of the drawn line. Cut the unit apart on the marked line to make two half-square-triangle units. Trim the units to 2" square, including seam allowances. Make eight units.

Make 8 units.

2. Repeat step 1 using the remaining marked white squares and the yellow squares to make eight half-square-triangle units measuring 2" square, including seam allowances.

Make 8 units.

3 Draw a diagonal line from corner to corner on the wrong side of eight white 2" squares. Place a marked square on one end of a green rectangle, right sides together and noting the orientation of the marked line. Sew on the marked line. Trim the excess corner fabric ¼" from the stitched line. Make four units. Reversing the orientation of the marked line, make four reversed units.

Make 4 of each unit,
2" × 3½".

4 Lay out two yellow half-square-triangle units and two white 2" squares in two rows of two, noting the orientation of the units. Sew the pieces into rows. Join the rows to make a corner unit measuring 3½" square, including seam allowances. Make four units.

Make 4 units,
3½" × 3½".

5 Join one unit from step 3 and one white rectangle to make a side unit. Join one reversed unit and one white rectangle to make a reversed side unit. The units should measure 3½" square, including seam allowances. Make four of each unit.

Make 4 of each unit,
3½" × 3½".

6 Lay out two green half-square-triangle units, one orange square, and one white 2" square in two rows of two. Sew the pieces into rows. Join the rows to make a base unit measuring 3½" square, including seam allowances. Make four units.

Make 4 units,
3½" × 3½".

7 Lay out the units from steps 4–6 in two rows of two, rotating the units as shown in the coaster assembly diagram below. Sew the units into rows. Join the rows to make a block measuring 6½" square, including seam allowances. Make four blocks.

8 Sew white 1" × 6½" strips to the top and bottom of each block. Sew white 1" × 7½" strips to the left and right sides of each block. Make four coasters measuring 7½" square.

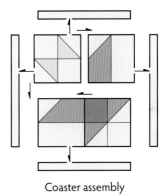

Coaster assembly

Finishing the Coasters

For more details on any finishing steps, visit ShopMartingale.com/HowtoQuilt for free downloadable information.

1 Layer each coaster with batting and backing; baste the layers together.

2 Quilt by hand or machine. The coasters shown are machine quilted with straight lines.

3 Use the green 2¼"-wide strips to make binding and then attach the binding to the coasters.

Liberty Hill

For the Fourth of July, I'm all about bringing out my red, white, and blue decorations! The classic blue-and-white color scheme can be displayed all summer long. For Liberty Hill, I looked to the sea. In a tribute to everyone who landed on our shores by boat, I used my nautical fabric collection. The block looks complicated but it's not!

 FINISHED QUILT: 56½" × 72½"
FINISHED BLOCK: 15" × 15"

Materials

Yardage is based on 42"-wide fabric. Fat quarters measure 18" × 21".

1¾ yards of white dot A for blocks and borders

1⅝ yards of white dot B for blocks and borders

⅞ yard of blue stripe for blocks, pieced border, and binding

¼ yard *each* of 4 different blue prints (A–D) for blocks and pieced border

⅓ yard *each* of 3 different blue prints (E–G) for blocks and pieced border

6 fat quarters of assorted light prints for blocks

3½ yards of fabric for backing

63" × 79" piece of batting

Cutting

All measurements include ¼" seam allowances.

From white dot A, cut:

- 8 strips, 3½" × 42"; crosscut into:
    24 rectangles, 3½" × 5"
    48 squares, 3½" × 3½"
- 1 strip, 3" × 42"; crosscut into 6 squares, 3" × 3"
- 7 strips, 2½" × 42"
- 3 strips, 2" × 42"; crosscut into 24 rectangles, 2" × 3½"

From white dot B, cut:

- 8 strips, 3½" × 42"; crosscut into:
    24 rectangles, 3½" × 5"
    48 squares, 3½" × 3½"
- 1 strip, 3" × 42"; crosscut into 6 squares, 3" × 3"
- 3 strips, 2½" × 42"
- 7 strips, 2" × 42"; crosscut *3 of the strips* into 24 rectangles, 2" × 3½"

From the blue stripe, cut:

- 3 strips, 3½" × 42"; crosscut into:
    16 rectangles, 3½" × 5"
    2 squares, 3" × 3"
    8 squares, 2" × 2"
- 7 strips, 2¼" × 42"

From *each* of blue prints A–D, cut:

- 2 strips, 3½" × 42"; crosscut into:
    8 rectangles, 3½" × 5" (32 total)
    1 square, 3" × 3" (4 total)
    4 squares, 2" × 2" (16 total)

From *each* of blue prints E–G, cut:

- 3 strips, 3½" × 42"; crosscut into:
    16 rectangles, 3½" × 5" (48 total)
    2 squares, 3" × 3" (6 total)
    8 squares, 2" × 2" (24 total)

From *each* of the assorted light prints, cut:

- 2 squares, 6½" × 6½" (12 total)
- 16 squares, 2" × 2" (96 total)

31

Making the Blocks

Instructions are for making one block; repeat to make a total of 12 blocks. Press seam allowances in the directions indicated by the arrows. For each block, select the following pieces.

From one white dot (either A or B):
- 4 rectangles, 3½" × 5"
- 4 rectangles, 2" × 3½"
- 8 squares, 3½" × 3½"

From one blue print:
- 8 rectangles, 3½" × 5"
- 4 squares, 2" × 2"

From one light print:
- 1 square, 6½" × 6½"
- 8 squares, 2" × 2"

1 Draw a diagonal line from corner to corner on the wrong side of the white 3½" and light 2" squares. Place a marked white square on one end of a blue rectangle, right sides together. Sew on the marked line. Trim the excess corner fabric ¼" from the stitched line. Set aside the trimmed blue and white triangles for step 3. Place a marked light square on the opposite end of the rectangle, noting the orientation of the marked line. Sew and trim as before to make a star-point unit measuring 3½" × 5", including seam allowances. Make four units.

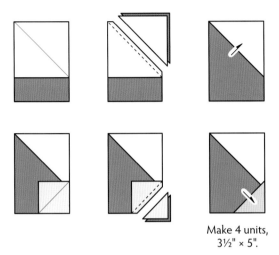

Make 4 units,
3½" × 5".

2 Repeat step 1, using the remaining marked white 3½" squares, light 2" squares, and four blue rectangles. Noting the orientation of the marked lines, make four reverse star-point units.

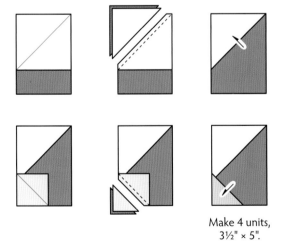

Make 4 units,
3½" × 5".

3 Using the blue triangles and white triangles set aside in steps 1 and 2, sew the triangles along their long edges to make 96 half-square-triangle units. Trim the units to 2½" square, including seam allowances. Set the units aside to make the pieced border.

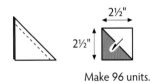

2½"

2½"

Make 96 units.

4 Join a star-point unit and a reverse star-point unit to make a side unit measuring 5" × 6½", including seam allowances. Make four units.

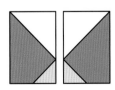 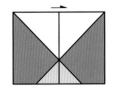

Make 4 units,
5" × 6½".

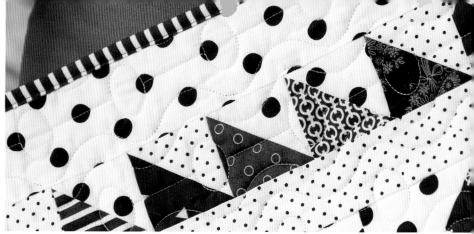

5 Join a blue square to the end of a white 2" × 3½" rectangle. Add a white 3½" × 5" rectangle to make a corner unit measuring 5" square, including seam allowances. Make two units. Reverse the orientation of the blue square to make two reversed corner units.

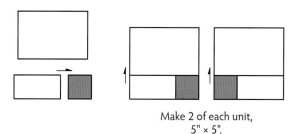

Make 2 of each unit,
5" × 5".

6 Lay out the corner units, the side units, and a light 6½" square in three rows, noting the orientation of the units. Sew the pieces into rows. Join the rows to make a block measuring 15½" square, including seam allowances. Repeat the steps to make a total of 12 blocks.

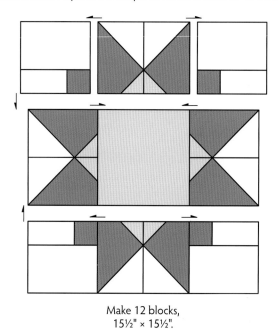

Make 12 blocks,
15½" × 15½".

Making the Pieced Border

1 Draw a diagonal line from corner to corner on the wrong side of the white dot A and B 3" squares. Layer a marked square on a blue 3" square, right sides together. Sew ¼" from both sides of the drawn line. Cut the unit apart on the marked line to make two half-square-triangle units. Trim the units to 2½" square, including seam allowances. Make 24 units. You should now have a total of 120 units (4 of the units will be extra).

Make 24 units.

2 Join 24 half-square-triangle units to make the top border. Repeat to make the bottom border. The borders should measure 2½" × 48½", including seam allowances. Join 34 units to make a side border, noting the orientation of the end units. Make two side borders measuring 2½" × 68½", including seam allowances.

Make 2 top/bottom borders,
2½" × 48½".

Make 2 side borders,
2½" × 68½".

FOURTH OF JULY

Assembling the Quilt Top

Refer to the quilt assembly diagram below as needed throughout.

1 Lay out the blocks in four rows of three blocks each. Sew the blocks into rows. Join the rows to make a quilt top measuring 45½" × 60½", including seam allowances.

2 Join the three white dot B 2½"-wide strips end to end. From the pieced strip, cut two 45½"-long strips and sew them to the top and bottom of the quilt top. Join the four remaining white dot B 2"-wide strips in pairs. From each pieced strip, cut one 64½"-long strip and sew these strips to opposite sides of the quilt top, which should be 48½" × 64½", including seam allowances.

3 Sew the shorter pieced borders to the top and bottom of the quilt top. Sew the longer pieced borders to opposite sides of the quilt top, which should be 52½" × 68½", including seam allowances.

4 Join the white dot A strips end to end. From the pieced strip, cut two 72½"-long strips and two 52½"-long strips. Sew the shorter strips to the top and bottom of the quilt top. Sew the longer strips to opposite sides of the quilt top, which should be 56½" × 72½".

Finishing the Quilt

For more details on any finishing steps, visit ShopMartingale.com/HowtoQuilt for free downloadable information.

1 Layer the quilt top with batting and backing; baste the layers together.

2 Quilt by hand or machine. The quilt shown is machine quilted with an allover pattern of wavy lines and circles.

3 Use the blue stripe 2¼"-wide strips to make binding and then attach the binding to the quilt.

Quilt assembly

Welcome Home

How sweet it is to hear those wonderful words, "Welcome home." To send a heartfelt message, hang an inviting quilt by your door or use it as a garden flag. For a housewarming gift, embroider the owner's house number above the door to make it more personal and extra special!

Materials

Yardage is based on 42"-wide fabric.

5" × 9" rectangle of navy print A for house

2" × 3" rectangle of navy print B for flag

3" × 4" rectangle of white print for windows

3" × 5" rectangle of blue print for door

6" × 6" square of yellow print A for sun

4" × 8" rectangle of yellow print B for sun rays

4" × 6" rectangle of yellow print C for butterfly wings

4" × 6" rectangle of red print A for roof

3" × 4" rectangle of red print B for heart

2" × 4" rectangle of red print C for butterfly body

6" × 6" square of red stripe for flag

¼ yard of navy solid for flagpole and binding

13½" × 18½" rectangle of light print for background

5" × 20" rectangle of green print for grass

⅝ yard of fabric for backing

21" × 23" piece of batting

⅝ yard of 16"-wide paper-backed fusible web

50-weight thread in colors to match appliqués

Cutting

All measurements include ¼" seam allowances.

From the navy solid, cut:
• 2 strips, 2¼" × 42"
• 1 rectangle, 1" × 13"

From the fusible web, cut:
• 1 square, 6" × 6"
• 1 rectangle, 5" × 9"
• 1 rectangle, 3" × 5"
• 1 rectangle, 3" × 4"
• 1 rectangle, 2" × 3"
• 1 rectangle, 1" × 13"

Preparing the Appliqués

You can learn more about my fusible-appliqué techniques in my book *Pat Sloan's Teach Me to Appliqué* (Martingale, 2015).

1 Following the manufacturer's instructions, fuse the 5" × 9" rectangle of fusible web to the wrong side of the navy A rectangle. Cut out one house, 4" × 8".

2 Fuse the 2" × 3" rectangle of fusible web to the wrong side of the navy B rectangle. Cut out one flag star section, 1½" × 2".

3 Fuse the 3" × 4" rectangle of fusible web to the wrong side of the white rectangle. Cut out three windows, 1" × 2".

4 Fuse the 3" × 5" rectangle of fusible web to the wrong side of the blue print. Cut out one door, 2" × 4½".

5 Fuse the 6" square of fusible web to the wrong side of the red stripe. Cut out one flag, 3" × 5", making sure the stripes run the length of the rectangle.

6 Fuse the 1" × 13" rectangle of fusible web to the wrong side of the navy solid rectangle. Cut out one flagpole, ½" × 12".

7 Using the patterns on pages 39 and 40, trace each shape the number of times indicated on the patterns onto the fusible web. Roughly cut out each shape, about ½" beyond the drawn line. For larger shapes, such as the sun, cut through the excess web around the shape, and then cut through the marked line and into the interior of the shape. Then cut away the excess fusible web on the *inside* of the shape, leaving less than ¼" inside the drawn line.

8 Position the fusible-web shapes on the fabrics indicated on the patterns. Fuse as instructed by the manufacturer. Cut out the shapes on the marked line and remove the paper backing from each shape.

Appliquéing the Quilt Top

1 Referring to the appliqué placement diagram, position the prepared appliqué shapes on the light rectangle starting with the bottommost layer (grass) and working toward the topmost layer (windows and heart).

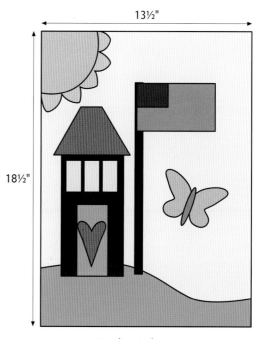

Appliqué placement

2 Fuse the appliqués in place. Blanket-stitch around the outer edge of each shape using matching thread.

Finishing the Quilt

For more details on any finishing steps, visit ShopMartingale.com/HowtoQuilt for free downloadable information.

1 Layer the quilt top with batting and backing; baste the layers together.

2 Quilt by hand or machine. The quilt shown is machine quilted with swirls and loops in the background; wavy lines in the grass; and swirls in the sun, butterfly wings, and flag. The appliqués are outline stitched.

3 Use the navy solid 2¼"-wide strips to make binding and then attach the binding to the quilt.

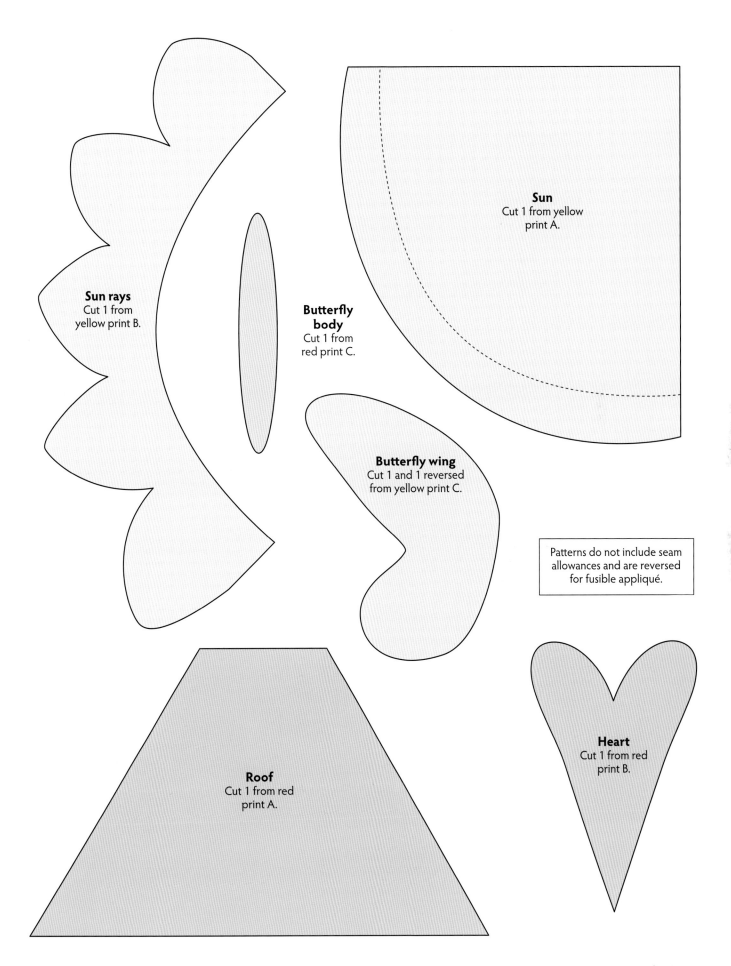

Sun
Cut 1 from yellow
print A.

Sun rays
Cut 1 from
yellow print B.

**Butterfly
body**
Cut 1 from
red print C.

Butterfly wing
Cut 1 and 1 reversed
from yellow print C.

Patterns do not include seam
allowances and are reversed
for fusible appliqué.

Heart
Cut 1 from red
print B.

Roof
Cut 1 from red
print A.

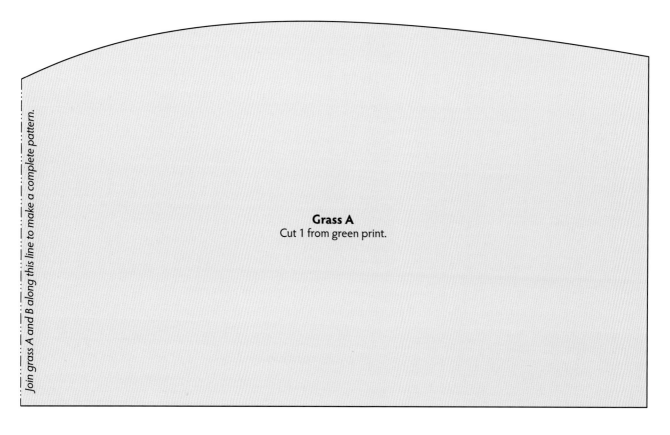

Join grass A and B along this line to make a complete pattern.

Grass A
Cut 1 from green print.

Patterns do not include seam
allowances and are reversed
for fusible appliqué.

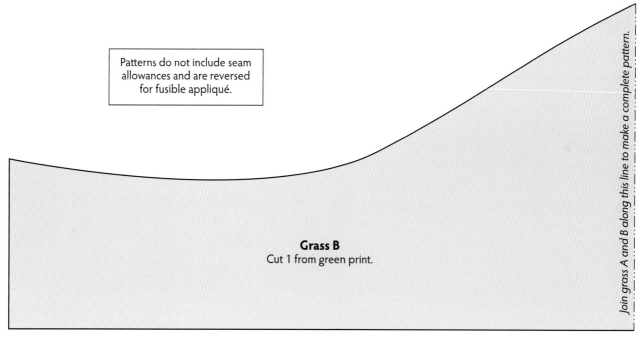

Join grass A and B along this line to make a complete pattern.

Grass B
Cut 1 from green print.

Sparklers

As the sun sets on the Fourth of July, it's fun to get ready for the fireworks. You've eaten hamburgers and hot dogs, played tag, and now settled into lawn chairs for the overhead display. As a child, I always got to light sparklers just as the sun was setting. That kept my attention until the real show started. Years later, I still like a handful of sparklers on the Fourth. You can celebrate all summer with a quilt that's the perfect size to top a picnic table or give to an Independence Day baby.

FINISHED QUILT: 54½" × 54½"
FINISHED BLOCK: 20" × 20"

Materials

Yardage is based on 42"-wide fabric. Fat quarters measure 18" × 21".

2 fat quarters, 1 *each* of 2 different red prints (A and B) for blocks

½ yard *each* of 4 assorted light prints (A–D) for blocks and ribbon border

2½ yards of blue solid for blocks, sashing, and borders

1 fat quarter of navy print for blocks

½ yard of red solid for binding

3½ yards of fabric for backing

61" × 61" piece of batting

Cutting

All measurements include ¼" seam allowances.

From *each* of red prints A and B, cut:
• 8 squares, 5" × 5" (16 total)

From light print A, cut:
• 8 squares, 5" × 5"
• 1 square, 3" × 3"
• 21 squares, 2½" × 2½"

Continued on page 43

Continued from page 41

From light print B, cut:
- 8 squares, 5" × 5"
- 1 square, 3" × 3"
- 20 squares, 2½" × 2½"

From light print C, cut:
- 8 squares, 4½" × 4½"
- 1 square, 3" × 3"
- 20 squares, 2½" × 2½"

From light print D, cut:
- 8 squares, 4½" × 4½"
- 1 square, 3" × 3"
- 24 squares, 2½" × 2½"

From the blue solid, cut:
- 3 strips, 5" × 42"; crosscut into:
    - 16 squares, 5" × 5"
    - 4 squares, 3" × 3"
- 4 strips, 4½" × 42"; crosscut into 16 rectangles, 4½" × 8½"
- 19 strips, 2½" × 42"; crosscut *9 of the strips* into:
    - 4 strips, 2½" × 20½"
    - 40 rectangles, 2½" × 4½"
    - 4 rectangles, 2½" × 3½"
    - 4 rectangles, 1½" × 2½"

From the navy print, cut:
- 4 squares, 4½" × 4½"

From the red solid, cut:
- 6 strips, 2¼" × 42"

Making the Blocks

Press seam allowances in the directions indicated by the arrows.

1 Draw a diagonal line from corner to corner on the wrong side of the red A, light A, and light B 5" squares.

2 Layer a marked red A square on a blue 5" square, right sides together. Sew ¼" from both sides of the drawn line. Cut the unit apart on the marked line to make two half-square-triangle units. Trim the units to 4½" square, including seam allowances. Make 16 units.

Make 16 units.

3 Repeat step 2 using the marked light B and blue 5" squares to make 16 units. Use the marked light A and red B squares to make 16 units.

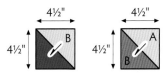

Make 16 units.   Make 16 units.

4 Sew one red A/blue unit, one blue/light B unit, one light A/red B unit, and one light D 4½" square into two rows. Sew the rows together to make a side unit measuring 8½" square, including seam allowances. Make eight units.

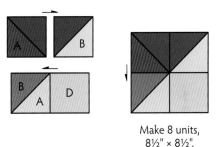

Make 8 units, 8½" × 8½".

5 Join one light A/red B unit, one red A/blue unit, and one blue 4½" × 8½" rectangle to make a corner unit measuring 8½" square, including seam allowances. Make eight units.

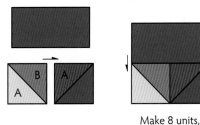

Make 8 units, 8½" × 8½".

TRIANGLE EASE

Pat's Pro Tip: All the pieces are cut slightly oversized so that you can trim your completed half-square-triangle units to the exact size. And that makes it easy to assemble the blocks and borders without trouble.

Making the Ribbon Border

1 Draw a diagonal line from corner to corner on the wrong side of the light A–D 2½" squares. Place a marked square on one end of a blue 2½" × 4½" rectangle, right sides together. Sew on the marked line. Trim the excess corner fabric ¼" from the stitched line. Place a marked square on the opposite end of the blue rectangle. Sew and trim as before to make a flying-geese unit measuring 2½" × 4½", including seam allowances. Make 40 units. You'll have one marked A and four marked D squares left over to use when assembling the quilt top.

Make 40 units,
2½" × 4½".

2 Draw a diagonal line from corner to corner on the wrong side of the light A–D 3" squares. Layer a marked square on a blue 3" square, right sides together. Sew ¼" from both sides of the drawn line. Cut the unit apart on the marked line to make two half-square-triangle units. Trim the units to 2½" square, including seam allowances. Make eight units.

Make 8 units.

3 Join 10 flying-geese units, two matching half-square-triangle units, and two blue 1½" × 2½" rectangles, noting the orientation of the units as shown on page 45, to make a side border measuring 2½" × 46½", including seam allowances. Make two borders. Join 10 flying-geese units, two matching

6 Lay out two side units, two corner units, two blue/light B units, two blue 4½" × 8½" rectangles, two light C 4½" squares, and one navy square in three rows, rotating the units as shown. Sew the pieces into rows. Join the rows to make a block measuring 20½" square, including seam allowances. Make four blocks.

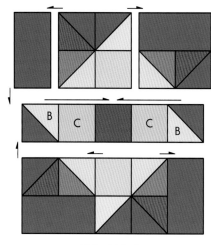

Make 4 blocks,
20½" × 20½".

FOURTH OF JULY

half-square-triangle units, and two blue 2½" × 3½" rectangles to make the top border measuring 2½" × 50½", including seam allowances. Repeat to make the bottom border.

Side borders.
Make 2 borders, 2½" × 46½".

Top/bottom borders.
Make 2 borders, 2½" × 50½".

Assembling the Quilt Top

Refer to the quilt assembly diagram at right as needed throughout.

1 Using the remaining four marked light D 2½" squares from step 1 of "Making the Ribbon Border," place a marked square on one end of a blue 2½" × 20½" strip, right sides together. Sew on the marked line. Trim the excess corner fabric ¼" from the stitched line. Repeat to make four sashing strips measuring 2½" × 20½", including seam allowances.

Make 4 strips,
2½" × 20½".

2 Lay out the blocks, sashing strips, and remaining light A 2½" square in three rows. Sew the pieces into rows. Join the rows to make a quilt top measuring 42½" square, including seam allowances.

3 Sew the blue 2½" strips end to end. From the pieced strips, cut two 54½"-long strips, two 50½"-long strips, two 46½"-long strips, and two 42½"-long strips.

4 Sew the blue 42½"-long strips to the sides of the quilt top. Sew the 46½"-long strips to the top and bottom of the quilt top, which should be 46½" square, including seam allowances.

5 Sew the shorter ribbon borders to the sides of the quilt top. Sew the longer ribbon borders to the top and bottom of the quilt top, which should be 50½" square, including seam allowances.

6 Sew the blue 50½"-long strips to the sides of the quilt top. Sew the 54½"-long strips to the top and bottom of the quilt top, which should be 54½" square.

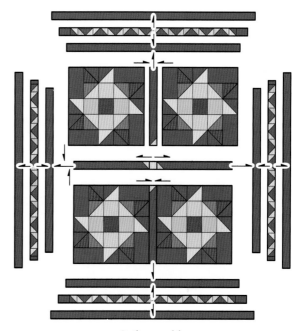

Quilt assembly

Finishing the Quilt

For more details on any finishing steps, visit ShopMartingale.com/HowtoQuilt for free downloadable information.

1 Layer the quilt top with batting and backing; baste the layers together.

2 Quilt by hand or machine. The quilt shown is machine quilted with straight lines in the blocks and a swirl design in the background and borders.

3 Use the red solid 2¼"-wide strips to make binding and then attach the binding to the quilt.

Spooky Twist

Decorating for Halloween has always been one of my favorite activities. I love jolly pumpkins and friendly ghosts. Toss in a hoot owl and a few spiderwebs in orange and black, and my trick-or-treat decorating is complete. Spooky Twist looks great in any holiday color—plus it's fast to assemble!

FINISHED QUILT: 36½" × 36½"
FINISHED BLOCK: 12" × 12"

Materials

Yardage is based on 42"-wide fabric.

⅝ yard of cream print for blocks

¾ yard of black print for blocks

1 yard of orange print for blocks and binding

2½ yards of fabric for backing

43" × 43" piece of batting

Cutting

All measurements include ¼" seam allowances.

From the cream print, cut:
• 4 strips, 5" × 42"; crosscut into 27 squares, 5" × 5"

From the black print, cut:
• 3 strips, 5" × 42"; crosscut into 18 squares, 5" × 5"
• 2 strips, 4½" × 42"; crosscut into 9 squares, 4½" × 4½"

From the orange print, cut:
• 4 strips, 5" × 42"; crosscut into 27 squares, 5" × 5"
• 4 strips, 2¼" × 42"

Making the Blocks

Press seam allowances in the directions indicated by the arrows.

1   Draw a diagonal line from corner to corner on the wrong side of the cream squares. Layer a marked square on a black 5" square, right sides together. Sew ¼" from both sides of the drawn line. Cut the unit apart on the marked line to make two half-square-triangle units. Trim the units to 4½" square, including seam allowances. Make 18 units.

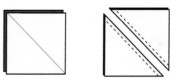

Make 18 units.

2   Repeat step 1 using the remaining marked cream squares and 18 of the orange squares to make 36 units. Draw a diagonal line from corner to corner on the wrong side of the remaining orange squares. Pair a marked orange square with a black 5" square to make 18 half-square-triangle units.

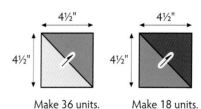

Make 36 units.   Make 18 units.

3 Lay out two black/cream units, four orange/cream units, two orange/black units, and one black 4½" square in three rows of three, noting the orientation of the units. Sew the units into rows. Join the rows to make a block measuring 12½" square, including seam allowances. Make nine blocks.

GET IT RIGHT

Arrange the half-square-triangle units into rows and then double-check to make sure they're positioned correctly before sewing. It's easy to twist one the wrong way.

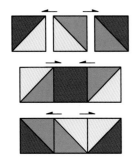

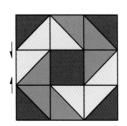

Make 9 blocks,
12½" × 12½".

HALLOWEEN

Assembling the Quilt Top

Lay out the blocks in three rows of three blocks each. Sew the blocks into rows. Join the rows. The quilt top should be 36½" square.

Finishing the Quilt

For more details on any finishing steps, visit ShopMartingale.com/HowtoQuilt for free downloadable information.

1 Layer the quilt top with batting and backing; baste the layers together.

2 Quilt by hand or machine. The quilt shown is machine quilted with straight lines in the cream areas. Loops and swirls are stitched in the orange and black patches.

3 Use the orange 2¼"-wide strips to make binding and then attach the binding to the quilt.

Quilt assembly

Trick-or-Treat

The trick-or-treaters are coming! When it's time to give candy to visiting goblins and ghosts on Halloween night, you can add to the excitement with a quilted bucket that's just the right size for tantalizing treats. Darling totes aren't just for kids! I use them to decorate my home. Hang a tote on a banister or doorknob and fill it with fall leaves. Use it to hold fabric scraps and supplies for small projects in the fall. Or hide candy in the tote for a special treat.

Candy Bucket

 FINISHED BUCKET: 10" diameter × 8" tall

Materials

Yardage is based on 42"-wide fabric.

⅛ yard *each* of 5 assorted light, medium, and dark Halloween prints (referred to collectively as "dark") for outer bucket

⅝ yard of black dot for outer bucket and lining

½ yard of single-sided fusible fleece

Cutting

All measurements include ¼" seam allowances.

From *each* of the dark prints, cut:
• 16 squares, 2½" × 2½" (80 total)

From the black dot, cut:
• 1 rectangle, 16½" × 25½"
• 16 squares, 2½" × 2½"

From the fusible fleece, cut:
• 2 rectangles, 12½" × 16½"

Making the Bucket

Press seam allowances in the directions indicated by the arrows.

1 Lay out the dark squares and black dot squares in six rows of eight squares each. Sew the squares into rows. Join the rows to make a front section measuring 12½" × 16½", including seam allowances. Repeat to make a back section.

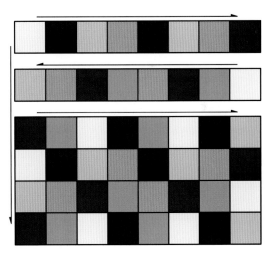

Make 2 sections,
12½" × 16½".

2 Fuse a rectangle of fusible fleece to the wrong side of both the front and back patchwork sections, following the manufacturer's instructions. Stitch a diagonal grid across the squares on each piece.

4 Fold the black dot rectangle in half, right sides together, to make a 12¾" × 16½" rectangle. Sew along both 12¾" side edges to make the lining.

5 With the wrong sides out, press the bottom corners of the lining and outer bucket flat to make a triangle. Draw a straight line perpendicular to the seam, 3½" in from each corner point. Sew along the line on both corners of the lining and outer bucket. Trim ¼" from the stitching line.

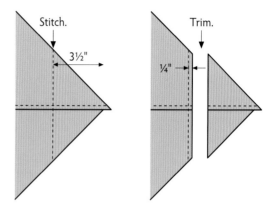

6 Turn the lining right side out. Place the lining inside the outer bucket, right sides together, aligning the side seams and top raw edges. Sew around the top edge, leaving a 5" opening for turning.

3 Layer the front and back sections right sides together with raw edges aligned. Starting and ending with a backstitch, sew around the side and bottom edges to make the outer bucket, making sure to leave the top edge open.

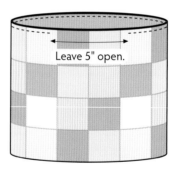

7 Turn the bucket right side out through the opening and push the lining into the bucket. Roll the lining to the exterior of the bucket so the lining makes a ¼" accent hem. Press. Topstitch around the folded edge of the lining to close the opening.

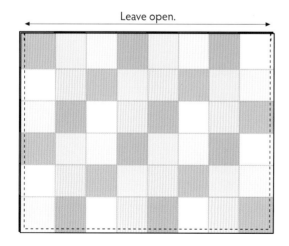

Treat Totes

FINISHED TOTE: 14" × 15", excluding handles

Materials

Yardage is based on 42"-wide fabric. Yields 2 totes.

1¼ yards of white print for blocks and lining

⅝ yard of black polka dot for blocks, tote back, and handles

⅝ yard of orange plaid for blocks, tote back, and handles

7" × 10" rectangle of orange tone on tone for pumpkin

5" × 6" rectangle of black small-scale dot for pumpkin eyes, nose, and mouth

3" × 3" square of brown print for pumpkin stem

8" × 8" square of white solid for ghost

5" × 5" square of purple A for bow

2" × 2" square of purple B for bow

2" × 3" rectangle of black solid for ghost eyes

1 yard of single-sided fusible fleece

½ yard of 16"-wide paper-backed fusible web

50-weight thread in colors to match appliqués

Cutting

All measurements include ¼" seam allowances.

From the white print, cut:
- 2 strips, 14½" × 42"; crosscut into 4 rectangles, 14½" × 15½" (lining)
- 1 strip, 9½" × 42"; crosscut into:
    - 1 rectangle, 9½" × 10½" (pumpkin tote)
    - 2 strips, 1½" × 12½" (ghost tote)
    - 2 strips, 1½" × 9½" (ghost tote)

From the black polka dot, cut:
- 1 strip, 15½" × 42"; crosscut into:
    - 1 rectangle, 14½" × 15½" (pumpkin tote)
    - 2 strips, 2" × 15½" (pumpkin tote)
    - 2 strips, 2" × 11½" (pumpkin tote)
    - 1 rectangle, 9½" × 10½" (ghost tote)
- 1 strip, 2½" × 42"; crosscut into 2 strips, 2½" × 20" (ghost tote)

From the orange plaid, cut:
- 1 strip, 15½" × 42"; crosscut into:
    - 1 rectangle, 14½" × 15½" (ghost tote)
    - 2 strips, 2" × 15½" (ghost tote)
    - 2 strips, 2" × 11½" (ghost tote)
    - 2 strips, 1½" × 12½" (pumpkin tote)
    - 2 strips, 1½" × 9½" (pumpkin tote)
- 1 strip, 2½" × 42"; crosscut into 2 strips, 2½" × 20" (pumpkin tote)

From the fusible fleece, cut:
- 4 rectangles, 14½" × 15½"

Making the Tote Fronts

Press seam allowances in the directions indicated by the arrows.

1 For the ghost tote, sew white 1½" × 9½" strips to the top and bottom and then sew white 1½" × 12½" strips to the sides of the black 9½" × 10½" rectangle. Sew orange 2" × 11½" strips to the top and bottom and then sew orange 2" × 15½" strips to the sides to make a tote front measuring 14½" × 15½".

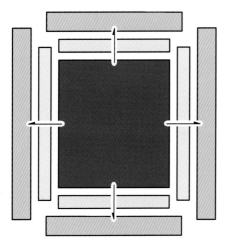

Make 1 tote front,
14½" × 15½".

2 For the pumpkin tote, sew orange 1½" × 9½" strips to the top and bottom and then sew orange 1½" × 12½" strips to the sides of the white 9½" × 10½" rectangle. Sew black 2" × 11½" strips to the top and bottom and then sew black 2" × 15½" strips to the sides to make a tote front measuring 14½" × 15½".

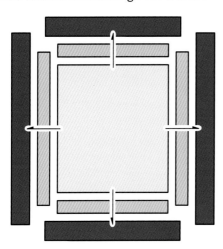

Make 1 tote front,
14½" × 15½".

Preparing the Appliqués

You can learn more about my fusible-appliqué techniques in my book *Pat Sloan's Teach Me to Appliqué* (Martingale, 2015).

1 Using the patterns on pages 56 and 57, trace each shape onto the fusible web. Roughly cut out each shape, about ½" beyond the drawn line. On large shapes, such as the ghost and pumpkin, cut through the excess web around the shape and through the marked line into the interior of the shape. Then cut away the excess fusible web on the *inside* of the shape, leaving less than ¼" inside the drawn line.

2 Position the fusible-web shapes on the fabrics indicated on the patterns. Fuse as instructed by the manufacturer. Cut out the shapes on the marked line and remove the paper backing from each shape.

3 Referring to the appliqué placement diagrams, position the prepared ghost shape on the tote front. Add the eyes and bow shapes. Position the prepared stem and pumpkin shapes on the tote front. Add the eyes, nose, and mouth to the pumpkin.

Appliqué placement   Appliqué placement

4 Fuse the appliqués in place. Blanket-stitch around the outer edge of each shape using matching thread.

Assembling the Totes

1 Fuse a rectangle of fusible fleece to the wrong side of each tote front, following the manufacturer's instructions. Outline stitch around the appliqués. Stitch meandering loops in the background and borders. Stitch curved lines on the pumpkin.

2 Fuse a rectangle of fusible fleece to the wrong side of the black and orange 14½" × 15½" rectangles. Machine quilt with meandering loops. These pieces are for the tote backs.

3 Place the ghost tote front and the orange tote back right sides together. Sew around the side and bottom edges, leaving the top open. Turn the tote right side out. In the same way, sew the pumpkin tote front to the black tote back.

4 Place two white 14½" × 15½" rectangles right sides together. Sew around the side and bottom edges as you did in step 3, leaving a 5" opening along the bottom edge. Do not turn the lining right side out. Make two.

5 To make the straps, fold over ¼" on each long edge of a black 2½" × 20" strip. Then fold the strip in half lengthwise, wrong sides together, and press. Topstitch along each long side of the strap a scant ⅛" from the edge. Repeat with the remaining black 2½" × 20" strip and the orange 2½" × 20" strips.

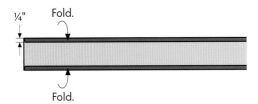

6 On the ghost tote front, mark 3½" in from each side seam along the top edge. With raw edges aligned, pin the ends of a black strap to the tote, aligning the outer edges of the strap with the 3½" mark. Repeat with the remaining black strap on the other side of the tote. In the same way, pin the orange straps to the front and back of the pumpkin tote.

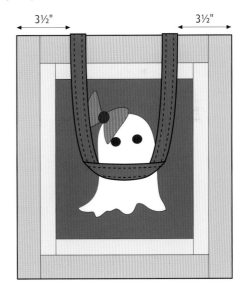

7 With right sides together, place an outer tote and strips inside the lining, sandwiching the straps between the layers. Align the raw edges and side seams; pin in place. Sew all the way around the top of the bag.

8 Pull the tote through the opening in the bottom seam of the lining. Sew the opening closed. Then push the lining into the tote.

9 Topstitch around the top edge of the tote, about ¼" from the edge. Repeat to complete the second tote.

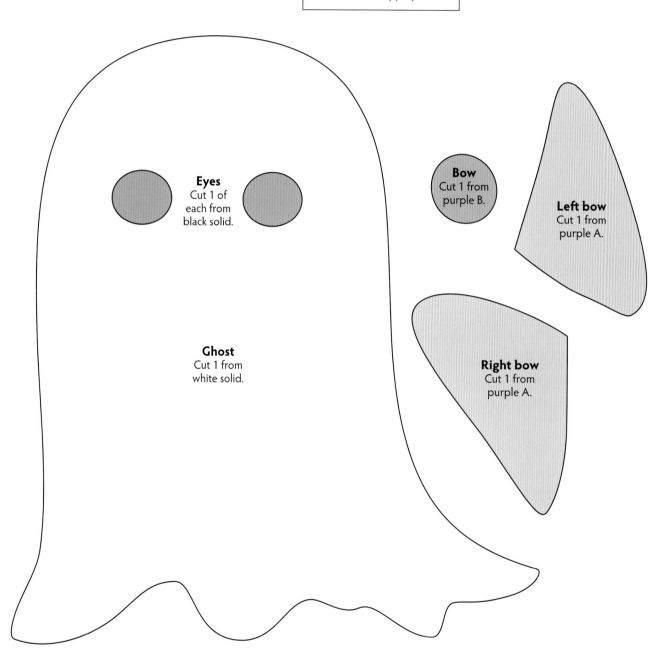

Patterns do not include seam allowances and are reversed for fusible appliqué.

Eyes
Cut 1 of each from black solid.

Bow
Cut 1 from purple B.

Left bow
Cut 1 from purple A.

Ghost
Cut 1 from white solid.

Right bow
Cut 1 from purple A.

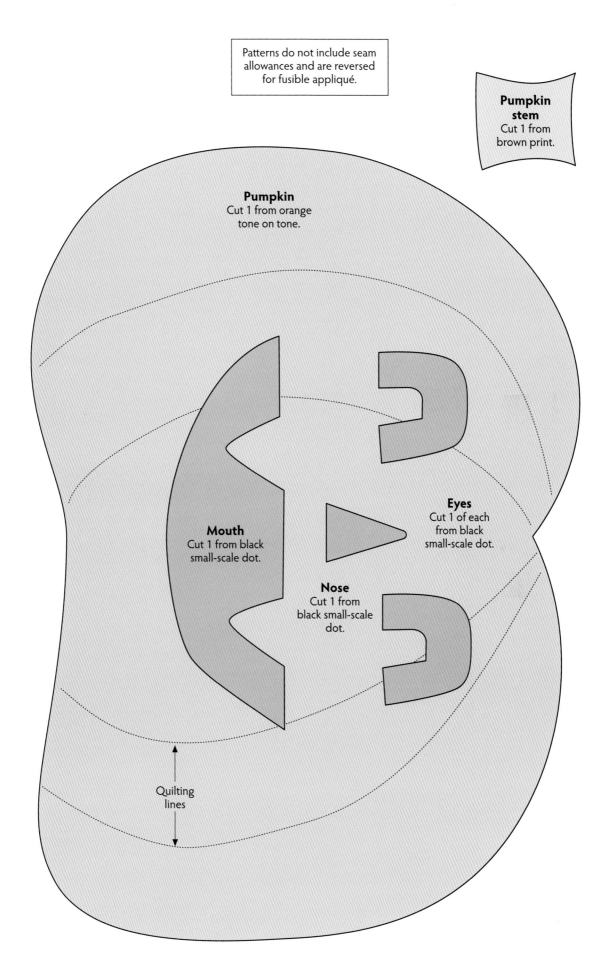

Patterns do not include seam allowances and are reversed for fusible appliqué.

Pumpkin stem
Cut 1 from brown print.

Pumpkin
Cut 1 from orange tone on tone.

Mouth
Cut 1 from black small-scale dot.

Eyes
Cut 1 of each from black small-scale dot.

Nose
Cut 1 from black small-scale dot.

Quilting lines

Give Thanks

Thanksgiving is my favorite holiday for so many reasons. We celebrate each other and give thanks. We enjoy a day that's about being together enjoying good food and good times. Thanksgiving also happens to land on my birthday every seven years or so, which adds to the fun!

FINISHED TABLE RUNNER: 16½" × 52½"
FINISHED BLOCK: 10" × 10"

Materials

Yardage is based on 42"-wide fabric.

1 yard of cream print for blocks, setting, and borders

½ yard of gray houndstooth for blocks and binding

⅛ yard *each* of 4 assorted gold prints for blocks

⅛ yard *each* of 4 assorted brown prints for blocks

1⅝ yards of fabric for backing

23" × 59" piece of batting

Cutting

All measurements include ¼" seam allowances.

From the cream print, cut:
- 2 strips, 4½" × 42"; crosscut into 5 rectangles, 4½" × 10½"
- 1 strip, 3¾" × 42"; crosscut into 10 squares, 3¾" × 3¾"
- 2 strips, 3" × 42"; crosscut into 20 squares, 3" × 3"
- 2 strips, 2½" × 42"; crosscut into:
    10 rectangles, 2½" × 4½"
    5 squares, 2½" × 2½"
- 4 strips, 1½" × 42"; crosscut *1 of the strips* into 2 strips, 1½" × 14½"

From the gray houndstooth, cut:
- 4 strips, 2¼" × 42"
- 5 squares, 4½" × 4½"

From the assorted gold prints, cut a *total* of:
- 10 squares, 3" × 3"
- 20 squares, 2½" × 2½"

From the assorted brown prints, cut a *total* of:
- 10 squares, 3" × 3"
- 20 squares, 2½" × 2½"

Making the Blocks

Press seam allowances in the directions indicated by the arrows.

1   Draw a diagonal line from corner to corner on the wrong side of the cream 3¾" squares. Place marked squares on opposite corners of a gray 4½" square. Sew on the marked lines. Trim the excess corner fabric ¼" from the stitched lines. Repeat to make five stem units measuring 4½" square, including seam allowances.

Make 5 units,
4½" × 4½".

2 Draw a diagonal line from corner to corner on the wrong side of the cream 3" squares. Layer a marked square on a gold or brown 3" square, right sides together. Sew ¼" from both sides of the drawn line. Cut the unit apart on the marked line to make two half-square-triangle units. Trim the units to 2½" square, including seam allowances. Make 40 units.

Make 40 units.

3 Lay out two cream 2½" × 4½" rectangles, four gold half-square-triangle units, four brown half-square-triangle units, four gold 2½" squares, four brown 2½" squares, one cream 2½" square, and one stem unit as shown. Sew the pieces into rows. Join the rows into sections and then join the sections to make a block measuring 10½" square, including seam allowances. Make five blocks.

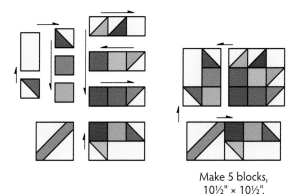

Make 5 blocks,
10½" × 10½".

Assembling the Table-Runner Top

1 Lay out the blocks and cream 4½" × 10½" rectangles in rows as shown in the table-runner assembly diagram on page 61. Sew the pieces into rows. Join the rows to make a table-runner center measuring 14½" × 50½", including seam allowances.

2 Sew the cream 1½" × 14½" strips to the ends of the table runner. Join the remaining cream 1½"-wide strips end to end. From the pieced strip cut two 52½"-long strips and sew them to the long edges of the table runner, which should be 16½" × 52½".

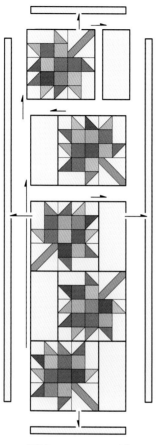

Table-runner assembly

Finishing the Table Runner

For more details on any finishing steps, visit ShopMartingale.com/HowtoQuilt for free downloadable information.

1. Layer the table-runner top with batting and backing; baste the layers together.

2. Quilt by hand or machine. The table runner shown is machine quilted in the ditch around each leaf and stem. A leaf motif is stitched in the center of each block. A continuous loop design is quilted throughout the background and border.

3. Use the gray 2¼"-wide strips to make binding and then attach the binding to the table runner.

NAPKINS

For a set of four napkins, you'll need 1½ yards of gray, ⅓ yard of gold, and ¼ yard of brown prints. For each coordinating napkin, cut 2 gray rectangles, 9½" × 14½", and 2 gray rectangles, 2½" × 14½". Cut 4 gold strips and 2 brown strips, each 1" × 14½". Join the strips and rectangles with the short gray rectangle on top, then the gold, brown, and gold strips, followed by the larger gray rectangle. (See photo above.) Make two of these pieced rectangles per napkin so that both sides of the napkin will match. Press both patchwork pieces, then lay them right sides together with the gold and brown strips aligned at the sides. Sew around the perimeter using a ¼" seam allowance and leaving a 4" opening for turning. Turn right sides out, press flat, and sew ⅛" from the outer edges to secure the opening and prevent the edges from shifting.

Hello, Autumn

What a joy it is to celebrate all the traditions of Thanksgiving. I prepare special food dishes, including some that I make only for this one holiday. Thanksgiving is also the day before the glitzy Christmas season starts. It won't be long before it's time to say farewell to fall and hello to winter!

Materials

Yardage is based on 42"-wide fabric.

⅓ yard of cream print for blocks, sashing, and border

⅛ yard of green print for blocks

¼ yard of gray floral for blocks and binding

⅛ yard *each* of gray and orange prints for blocks

⅛ yard of orange stripe for blocks

⅝ yard of fabric for backing

20" × 20" piece of batting

Cutting

All measurements include ¼" seam allowances.

From the cream print, cut:
- 1 strip, 3" × 42"; crosscut into:
    - 8 squares, 3" × 3"
    - 4 squares, 2½" × 2½"
- 1 strip, 2" × 42"; crosscut into 8 squares, 2" × 2"
- 3 strips, 1½" × 42"; crosscut into:
    - 2 strips, 1½" × 15½"
    - 2 strips, 1½" × 13½"
    - 4 strips, 1½" × 6½"

From the green print, cut:
- 4 squares, 2½" × 2½"
- 1 square, 1½" × 1½"

From the gray floral, cut:
- 2 strips, 2¼" × 42"
- 2 squares, 3" × 3"
- 4 squares, 2½" × 2½"

From *each* of the gray and orange prints, cut:
- 2 squares, 3" × 3" (4 total)
- 2 squares, 2½" × 2½" (4 total)

From the orange stripe, cut:
- 2 squares, 3" × 3"
- 4 squares, 2½" × 2½"

Making the Blocks

Press seam allowances in the directions indicated by the arrows.

1. Draw a diagonal line from corner to corner on the wrong side of the cream 2" squares. Place marked squares on opposite corners of a green 2½" square. Sew on the marked lines. Trim the excess corner fabric ¼" from the stitched lines. Repeat to make four stem units, 2½" square, including seam allowances.

Make 4 units,
2½" × 2½".

2. Draw a diagonal line from corner to corner on the wrong side of the cream 3" squares. Layer a marked square on a gray floral 3" square, right sides together. Sew ¼" from both sides of the drawn line. Cut the unit apart on the marked line to make two half-square-triangle units. Trim the units to 2½" square, including seam allowances. Make four gray floral units.

Make 4 units.

3. Repeat step 2 using marked cream squares and the gray print 3" squares to make four gray print units. Repeat using marked cream squares and the orange print 3" squares to make four orange print units. Use the remaining marked cream squares and the orange stripe 3" squares to make four orange stripe units.

Make 4 units.   Make 4 units.   Make 4 units.

Assembling the Table-Mat Top

1 Lay out the blocks, cream 1½" × 6½" strips, and green 1½" square in three rows as shown in the table-mat assembly diagram below. Sew the pieces into rows. Join the rows. The table mat should be 13½" square, including seam allowances.

2 Sew the cream 1½" × 13½" strips to opposite sides of the table mat. Sew the cream 1½" × 15½" strips to the top and bottom of the table mat, which should be 15½" square.

4 Lay out two gray floral units, two gray print units, one cream 2½" square, one gray print 2½" square, two gray floral 2½" squares, and one stem unit in three rows of three. Sew the pieces into rows. Join the rows to make a block measuring 6½" square, including seam allowances. Make two blocks.

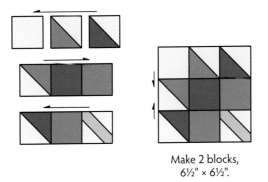

Make 2 blocks,
6½" × 6½".

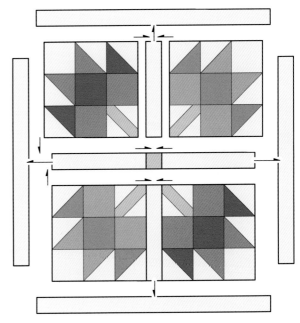

Table-mat assembly

5 Lay out two orange stripe units, two orange print units, one cream 2½" square, one orange print 2½" square, two orange stripe 2½" squares, and one stem unit in three rows of three. Sew the pieces into rows. Join the rows to make a block measuring 6½" square, including seam allowances. Make two blocks.

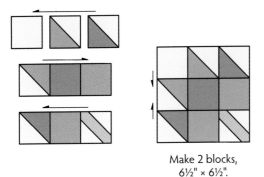

Make 2 blocks,
6½" × 6½".

Finishing the Table Mat

For more details on any finishing steps, visit ShopMartingale.com/HowtoQuilt for free downloadable information.

1 Layer the table-mat top with batting and backing; baste the layers together.

2 Quilt by hand or machine. The table mat shown is machine quilted with a flower and leaf motif in the center of each block. Wavy lines are stitched in the sashing strips and border.

3 Use the gray floral 2¼"-wide strips to make binding and then attach the binding to the table mat.

Merry Little Houses

From twinkling lights in the windows to a warm glow in the fireplace, there's no place like home at Christmastime. I enjoy collecting special novelty prints, so I gave each window a different print. Some of my scraps were just big enough for a window. Using a different red print for each house is also a fun way to create a scrappy quilt!

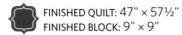 **FINISHED QUILT:** 47" × 57½"
FINISHED BLOCK: 9" × 9"

Materials

Yardage is based on 42"-wide fabric. Fat eighths measure 9" × 21".

1½ yards of white print for blocks, sashing, and borders

¼ yard *each* of 3 assorted green prints for blocks and outer border

20 fat eighths of assorted red prints for blocks

20 squares, 3½" × 3½" *each*, of assorted novelty prints for blocks

¼ yard of cream print for blocks

⅛ yard of snowflake print for sashing squares*

½ yard of red dot for binding

3 yards of fabric for backing

53" × 64" piece of batting

*If you want to fussy cut the squares, as I did, you may need more yardage.

Cutting

All measurements include ¼" seam allowances.

From the white print, cut:
- 4 strips, 3½" × 42"; crosscut into:
  40 squares, 3½" × 3½"
  2 squares, 3" × 3"
- 8 strips, 2" × 42"; crosscut into 31 strips, 2" × 9½"
- 4 strips, 2½" × 42"; crosscut into:
  2 strips, 2½" × 33½"
  2 strips, 2½" × 23"
- 5 strips, 1½" × 42"

From the green prints, cut a *total* of:
- 20 rectangles, 3½" × 9½"
- 2 squares, 3" × 3"

From *each* of the red prints, cut:
- 1 rectangle, 2½" × 9½" (20 total)
- 1 rectangle, 1½" × 5½" (20 total)
- 1 rectangle, 2½" × 4½" (20 total)
- 2 rectangles, 1½" × 3½" (40 total)

From the cream print, cut:
- 3 strips, 2½" × 42"; crosscut into 20 rectangles, 2½" × 4½"

From the snowflake print, cut:
- 12 squares, 2" × 2"

From the red dot, cut:
- 6 strips, 2¼" × 42"

Making the Blocks

Press seam allowances in the directions indicated by the arrows.

1. Draw a diagonal line from corner to corner on the wrong side of the white 3½" squares. Place marked square on both ends of a green rectangle, right sides together. Sew on the marked lines. Trim the excess corner fabric ¼" from the stitched lines. Use a rotary cutter and ruler to trim accurately, as you'll be using these leftover triangles for the quilt border. Make 20 roof units measuring 3½" × 9½", including seam allowances.

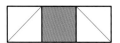 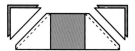

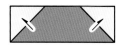

Make 20 units,
3½" × 9½".

2. Lay out one red 2½" × 9½" rectangle, two red 1½" × 3½" rectangles, one red 1½" × 5½" rectangle, one red 2½" × 4½" rectangle, one novelty print square, and one cream rectangle as shown. The red rectangles should all match. Join the pieces to make a house unit measuring 6½" × 9½", including seam allowances. Make 20 units.

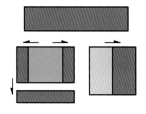 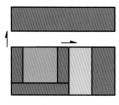

Make 20 units,
6½" × 9½".

3. Join one roof and one house unit to make a block measuring 9½" square, including seam allowances. Make 20 blocks.

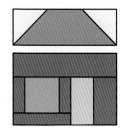 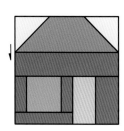

Make 20 blocks,
9½" × 9½".

Assembling the Quilt Top

Refer to the quilt assembly diagram below as needed throughout.

1 Join four house blocks and three white 2" × 9½" strips to make a block row measuring 9½" × 41", including seam allowances. Make five rows.

2 Join four white 2" × 9½" strips and three snowflake squares to make a sashing row measuring 2" × 41", including seam allowances. Make four rows.

3 Join the block rows alternately with the sashing rows to make the quilt-top center, which should measure 41" × 51½", including seam allowances.

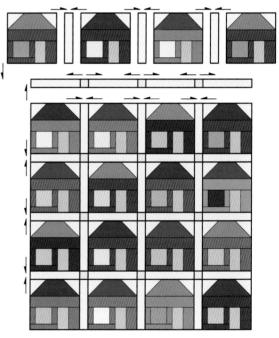

Quilt assembly

Adding the Borders

1 Join the white 1½" × 42" strips end to end. From the pieced strip, cut two 53½"-long strips and two 41"-long strips. Sew the shorter strips to the top and bottom of the quilt top. Sew the longer strips to opposite sides of the quilt top, which should be 43" × 53½", including seam allowances.

2 Using the trimmed triangles from making the roof units on page 67, join white and green triangles along their long edges to make a half-square-triangle unit. Trim the unit to 2½" square, including seam allowances. Make 40 units.

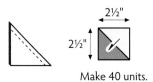

2½"
2½"

Make 40 units.

3 Draw a diagonal line from corner to corner on the wrong side of the white 3" squares. Layer a marked square on a green square, right sides together. Sew ¼" from both sides of the drawn line. Cut the unit apart on the marked line to make two half-square-triangle units. Trim the units to 2½" square, including seam allowances. Make four units. You will now have a total of 44 half-square-triangle units.

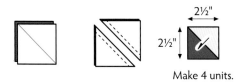

2½"
2½"

Make 4 units.

4 Join 10 half-square-triangle units and a white 2½" × 23" strip, noting the orientation of the units, to make a top border measuring 2½" × 43", including seam allowances. Repeat to make the bottom border. Join 12 half-square-triangle units and a white 2½" × 33½" strip to make a side border measuring 2½" × 57½", including seam allowances. Make two borders.

Top/bottom borders.
Make 2 borders, 2½" × 43".

Side borders.
Make 2 borders, 2½" × 57½".

5 Sew the top and bottom borders to the quilt top. Sew the side borders to opposite sides of the quilt top, which should be 47" × 57½".

Adding the borders

Finishing the Quilt

For more details on any finishing steps, visit ShopMartingale.com/HowtoQuilt for free downloadable information.

1 Layer the quilt top with batting and backing; baste the layers together.

2 Quilt by hand or machine. The quilt shown is machine quilted with an allover design of swirls and snowflakes.

3 Use the red dot 2¼"-wide strips to make binding and then attach the binding to the quilt.

Peppermint Twist

Oh, the sweet and tingly taste of peppermint—Christmas just wouldn't be the same without it. Celebrate a favorite candy as well as a classic color combination with a table runner that's sure to add zest to your holiday decor. Set a bowl of peppermint candies on top and enjoy!

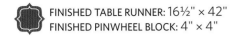 FINISHED TABLE RUNNER: 16½" × 42"
FINISHED PINWHEEL BLOCK: 4" × 4"

Materials

Yardage is based on 42"-wide fabric. Fat quarters measure 18" × 21".

4 fat quarters, 1 *each* of assorted white prints for blocks

4 fat quarters, 1 *each* of assorted red prints for blocks

2 fat quarters, 1 *each* of white solid and red solid for peppermint appliqués

1 fat quarter of white dot for appliqué background

1 fat quarter of red stripe for sashing

⅓ yard of red solid for binding

1⅓ yards of fabric for backing

23" × 48" piece of batting

½ yard of 16"-wide paper-backed fusible web

50-weight thread in colors to match appliqués

Cutting

All measurements include ¼" seam allowances.

From *each* of the assorted white prints, cut:
• 2 strips, 3" × 21"; crosscut into 12 squares, 3" × 3" (48 total)

From *each* of the assorted red prints, cut:
• 2 strips, 3" × 21"; crosscut into 12 squares, 3" × 3" (48 total)

From the white dot, cut:
• 2 strips, 5½" × 16½"

From the red stripe, cut:
• 5 strips, 2" × 16½"

From the red solid for binding, cut:
• 4 strips, 2¼" × 42"

Making the Pinwheel Blocks

Press seam allowances in the directions indicated by the arrows.

1 Draw a diagonal line from corner to corner on the wrong side of the white 3" squares. Layer a marked square on a red square, right sides together. Sew ¼" from both sides of the drawn line. Cut the unit apart on the marked line to make two half-square-triangle units. Trim the units to 2½" square, including seam allowances. Make 96 units.

Make 96 units.

2 Lay out four matching half-square-triangle units in two rows of two to form a pinwheel. Sew the units into rows. Join the rows to make a Pinwheel block measuring 4½" square, including seam allowances. Make 24 blocks.

Make 24 blocks, 4½" × 4½".

Making the Appliqué Borders

You can learn more about my fusible-appliqué techniques in my book *Pat Sloan's Teach Me to Appliqué* (Martingale, 2015). Press seam allowances in the directions indicated by the arrows.

1 Using the patterns on page 73, trace each shape onto the fusible web the number of times indicated on the patterns. Roughly cut out each shape, about ½" beyond the drawn line. On the circle only, cut through the excess web around the circle, through the marked line, and into the interior of the circle. Then cut away the excess fusible web on the *inside* of the circle, leaving less than ¼" inside the drawn line.

2 Position the fusible-web shapes on the fabrics indicated on the patterns. Fuse as instructed by the manufacturer. Cut out the shapes on the marked line and remove the paper backing from each shape.

3 Referring to the appliqué placement diagram, position three prepared fabric circles on a white dot strip. Place five swirl shapes on top of each white circle. Repeat to make a second border.

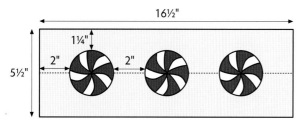

Appliqué placement

4 Fuse the appliqués in place. Blanket-stitch around the outer edge of each shape, alternating the color of thread to match the color of the fabric shapes so the stitching doesn't show.

Assembling the Table Runner

Refer to the table-runner assembly diagram below as needed throughout.

1 Join four Pinwheel blocks to make a column measuring 4½" × 16½", including seam allowances. Make six columns.

2 Join the block columns alternately with the red stripe strips. Sew an appliquéd border to each end of the table runner. The table runner should measure 16½" × 42".

Table-runner assembly

CHRISTMAS

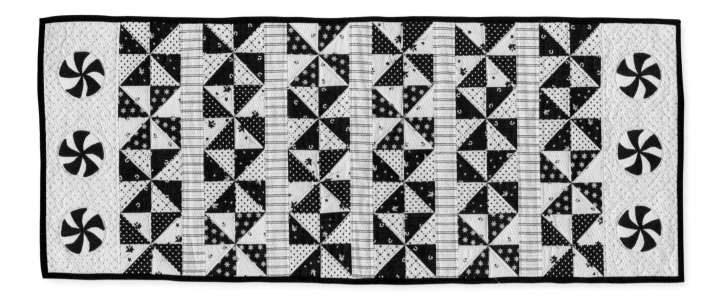

Finishing the Table Runner

For more details on any finishing steps, visit ShopMartingale.com/HowtoQuilt for free downloadable information.

1 Layer the table-runner top with batting and backing; baste the layers together.

2 Quilt by hand or machine. The table runner shown is machine quilted with straight lines along the seamlines in the blocks and sashing strips. A continuous loop design is stitched in the background of the appliquéd blocks.

3 Use the red solid 2¼"-wide strips to make binding and then attach the binding to the table runner.

REDUCE THE BULK

While I prefer to press seam allowances to one side, all the Pinwheel blocks in this quilt add up to a lot of seam allowances coming together when joining the blocks. So, you might consider pressing the seam allowances open on the Pinwheels before joining them. Or, try pressing the seam allowances open where two blocks come together to reduce the bulk in each row.

Patterns do not include seam allowances and are reversed for fusible appliqué.

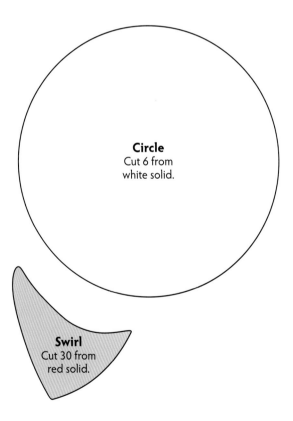

Circle
Cut 6 from white solid.

Swirl
Cut 30 from red solid.

Patchwork Stockings

Stockings are one of my favorite parts of Christmas morning. They hang empty for weeks, but we peek inside just in case. Then that morning we rush to enjoy them before we do anything else. It's so fun to find all the little treasures inside! Enjoy these quick-to-stitch stockings on your mantel or staircase banner with added greenery.

FINISHED STOCKINGS : 6" × 18"

Materials

Yardage is based on 42"-wide fabric. Fat quarters measure 18" × 21". Yields 2 stockings.

6 fat quarters of assorted prints for stocking fronts

¾ yard *each* of black plaid and red plaid for lining

⅜ yard *each* of 2 coordinating prints for stocking backs

4 pieces, 12" × 24" each, of batting

½ yard of ⅜"-wide grosgrain ribbon

3 sheets of copy paper

Permanent marker

Walking foot for your sewing machine

Cutting

All measurements include ¼" seam allowances.

CUTTING FOR STRIPED STOCKING

From *each* of the assorted fat quarters, cut:
• 1 rectangle, 2½" × 12½" (6 total)
• 1 rectangle, 2½" × 9½" (6 total)

From the black plaid, cut:
• 2 rectangles, 12" × 24"

From *1* of the coordinating prints, cut:
• 1 rectangle, 12" × 24"

CUTTING FOR CHECKERBOARD STOCKING

From *each* of the 6 fat quarters, cut:
• 11 squares, 2½" × 2½" (66 total; 3 are extra)

From the red plaid, cut:
• 2 rectangles, 12" × 24"

From *1* of the coordinating prints, cut:
• 1 rectangle, 12" × 24"

Making the Stocking Fronts and Backs

1 For the striped stocking, join the print 2½" × 9½" strips to make the top section. Join the print 2½" × 12½" strips to make the bottom section. Join the two sections, offsetting the top section as shown.

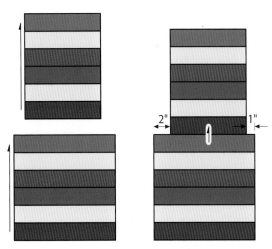

Make 1 unit.

2 For the checkerboard stocking, lay out the print squares in 11 rows as shown. Sew the squares into rows. Join the rows, offsetting the top three rows.

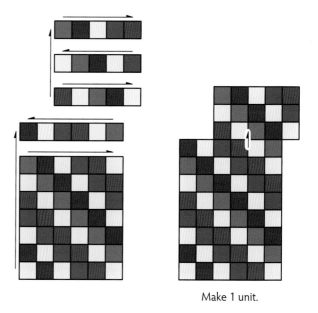

Make 1 unit.

3 Tape three pieces of paper together to make a piece measuring 11" × 24". Trace the stocking toe pattern on page 79 on one end of the paper. Using a ruler and starting at the placement line on the pattern, draw a rectangle measuring 6½" × 14½" to make the top of the stocking pattern. Cut out the stocking pattern directly on the drawn lines.

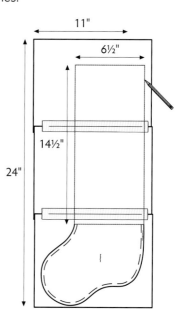

4 To make the striped stocking front, trace the stocking pattern onto the right side of the strip unit from step 1. Layer the strip unit with batting and a black plaid rectangle. Machine quilt straight lines along the seamlines. Cut out the stocking front on the marked line.

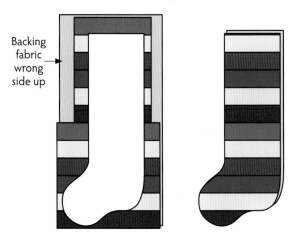

Backing fabric wrong side up

5 To make the striped stocking back, flip the stocking pattern over and trace the reverse stocking onto the right side of the remaining black plaid rectangle. Layer with batting and the coordinating 12" × 24" rectangle. Machine quilt evenly spaced straight lines. Cut out the stocking back on the marked line.

6 Repeat step 4 using the checkerboard unit from step 2 and a red plaid rectangle. Machine quilt diagonally across the squares in both directions. Cut out the stocking front on the marked line.

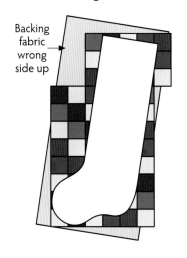

Backing fabric wrong side up

7 Repeat step 5 using the remaining red plaid rectangle and the coordinating 12" × 24" rectangle. Machine quilt a diagonal grid. Cut out the stocking back on the marked line.

Assembling the Stockings

1 On each stocking back, fold over ¼" along the top edge. Press and topstitch.

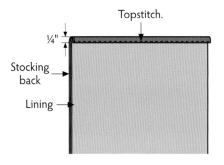

Topstitch.

¼"

Stocking back

Lining

2 On each stocking front, fold over 1/4" along the top edge. Press and topstitch. Then fold the top edge over 3" onto the stocking front. Pin in place.

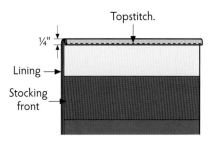

Topstitch.

¼"

Lining

Stocking front

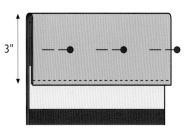

3"

3 Place a stocking front and stocking back (with matching lining) right sides together; align the raw edges. The back will be longer than the front. Fold the top of the back over the front. Use clips to secure the edges.

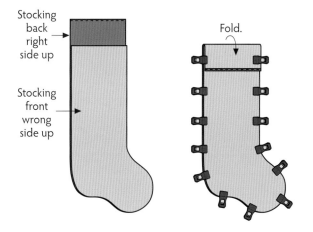

Stocking back right side up

Stocking front wrong side up

Fold.

4 Using a walking foot and starting at the top edge, sew around the stocking. Clip the curves to the stitched line.

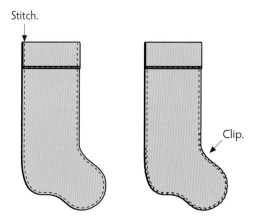

Stitch.

Clip.

5 Unfold the top of the stocking back and then turn the stocking right side out through the opening. Cut the ribbon into two pieces, each 9" long. Fold one piece in half and sew it to the inside back seam for the hanging loop.

6 Repeat steps 3–5 to make the second stocking.

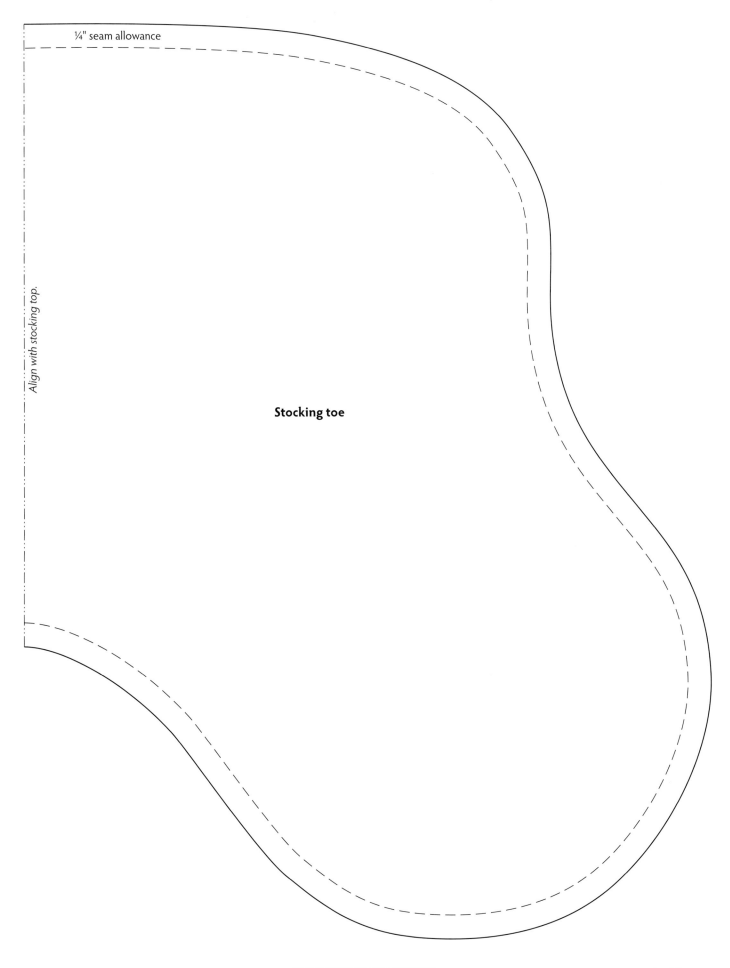

¼" seam allowance

Align with stocking top.

Stocking toe

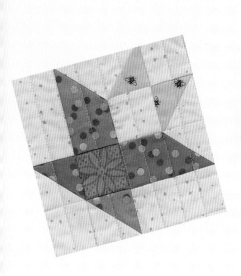

ACKNOWLEDGMENTS

A huge thank-you goes to my friends who helped out on these projects—Melanie Barrett, Judy Clark, and Cindy and Dennis Dickinson. Another huge thank-you goes to my wonderful business partners—Aurifil (thread), Mountain Mist (batting), Baby Lock (machines), OLFA (cutters), and Benartex (fabric).

About the Author

I'm a quilt designer, author, teacher, YouTuber, and fabric designer. My passion is to make quilting fun for everyone. I love to make quilts, share quilts, and talk about quilts. I host a very active, friendly, and exciting quilting community on Facebook called Quilt Along with Pat Sloan. I host lots of sew-alongs and challenges, and we have so much fun! Find me at PatSloan.com and sign up for my notices. I can't wait to chat with you!